Standards Based Grammar

Grade 3

By David S. Dye M.Ed.

Student Edition

MODEL
CITIZEN
PUBLICATIONS

Model Citizen Publications,
Long Beach, CA 90808

This book is dedicated to my mother, Delores,
who is the hardest working person I've ever known...

...and to my wife, Joy, who is the most
loving, supportive person I've ever known.

For workshop / staff development information call
(562) 627-5662 or go to CreateBetterWriters.com.

ISBN-13: 9781500737382   ISBN-10: 1500737380

Table of Contents

_____

Student Name

		Mastery	Non-Mastery
	1. Parts of Speech: Noun Definitions and ID – Unit 1		
	2. Parts of Speech: Possessive Nouns – Unit 1		
	3. Parts of Speech: Plural Noun Spelling Rules – Unit 1		
	4. Capitalization – Unit 2		
	5. Parts of Speech: Pronouns – Unit 3		
	6. Parts of Speech: Verbs – Unit 3 (Past, Present, and Future)		
	7. Parts of Speech: Adjectives – Unit 3		
	8. Parts of Speech: Contractions – Unit 3		
	9. Comma Rules: Dates – Unit 4		
	10. Comma Rules: City, State / Addresses – Unit 4		
	11. Comma Rules: Lists – Unit 4		
	12. Comma Rules: Adjectives – Unit 4		
	13. Comma Rules: Letters – Unit 4		
	14. Four (4) Types of Sentences – Unit 5		
	15. Subjects and Predicates – Unit 5		
	16. Finding Subjects and Predicates – Unit 5		
	17. Phrases – Unit 6		
	18. Fragment and Run-On Sentences – Unit 6		
	19. Title or Topic Sentence? – Unit 6		
	20. Subject-Verb Agreement – Unit 6		
	21. Homonyms – Unit 7		
	22. Compound Words – Unit 7		
	23. A vs. An – Unit 7		
	24. Friendly Letters – Unit 8		
	25. Using Prefixes and Suffixes to Determine Meaning – Unit 9 un, re, pre, bi , mis, dis er est ful		
	26. Using Suffixes – Unit 9 er est ful		

Unit 1

Parts of Speech: Nouns

Noun Definition and Identification

Possessive Nouns

Plural Noun Rules

_____
Student

Parts of Speech

	Mastery	Non-Mastery
1. Noun Definitions and Identification		
2. Possessive Nouns		
3. Plural Noun Spelling Rules		

Nouns
Definitions
#1

In the next few chapters there are going to be many new words to memorize. Use the tricks recommended on the following pages to help you remember them all.

Nouns
The name of a person, place, or thing.

The Trick:
1. The word "noun" sounds like "nun." When you think of a noun, think of a nun.
2. A noun is a person, place, or thing. Think of a nun (person) going to a church (place) wearing a ring (thing).

In the space below, draw a nun in front of a church wearing a ring. Write the word "person" next to the nun, "place" next to the church, and "thing" next to the ring.

Chant: **"The nun went to the church wearing a ring: person, place, or thing."**

Directions: Write "person", "place", or "thing" next to each noun.

1. nun - _____
2. church - _____
3. ring - _____
4. park - _____
5. bike - _____
6. coach - _____
7. computer - _____
8. store - _____
9. driver - _____
10. school - _____
11. friend - _____
12. watch - _____

Nouns
Definitions
#2

Write the definition of a noun. Remember the trick.

Common Nouns

Common nouns DO NOT name exact people, places or things.

girl, teacher, house, dog

The Trick:
Draw several nuns in a park. We do not know any of their names.

Common Nuns

Proper Nouns

Proper nouns name EXACT people, places, or things.

Amy, Mrs. Jones, White House, Fido

The Trick:
Draw a nun. Call her "Sister Mary". This is the exact name of the nun.

Sister Mary, the Proper Nun

Directions: Underline all of the nouns in the sentences below. Write "common" or "proper" above each noun.

1. Sister Mary gave graduation rings to Alejandra and Juan.

2. Our dog barked at Mrs. Ly, our neighbor.

3. His family went to San Francisco and drove their car across the Golden Gate Bridge.

4. Simm's Park will have a Halloween party and give away a lot of candy.

5. Mrs. Jones gave everyone in our class some pencils, paper, and folders.

Nouns
Definitions
#3

Write the definitions of common and proper nouns. Remember the tricks.

Common Nouns: _____

Proper Nouns: _____

I. Write a common noun for each proper noun below.

1. Sarah - _____**girl**_____   6. Mrs. Jones - _____

2. Arizona - _____   7. Jones Bikes Shop - _____

3. Bugs Bunny - _____   8. Bible - _____

4. Olympics - _____   9. General Franks - _____

5. Grand Canyon - _____   10. Los Angeles - _____

II. Write a proper noun for each common noun below.

1. boy - _____   6. country - _____

2. dog - _____   7. song - _____

3. principal - _____   8. car - _____

4. actor - _____   9. name - _____

5. athlete - _____   10. store - _____

III. Write "Common" or "Proper" next to each noun.

1. BANANA - _____   6. DESERT - _____

2. TEXAS - _____   7. ENGLAND - _____

3. TIGER - _____   8. FARM - _____

4. DR. GEORGE - _____   9. MONOPOLY(game) - _____

5. DANIEL - _____   10. DRIVER - _____

Extension: Make a list of five (5) proper nouns. Write a matching common noun next to the proper noun just like in Part I above.

Nouns
Definitions
#4

Write the definitions of common and proper nouns. Remember the tricks.

Common Nouns: _____

Proper Nouns: _____

I. Write a common noun for each proper noun below.

1. Alexander - _____   6. Dr. Lee - _____

2. Mojave Desert - _____   7. Susie's Deli - _____

3. Porky Pig - _____   8. Frisbee - _____

4. Rose Parade - _____   9. Colonel Sanders - _____

5. White House - _____   10. Jupiter - _____

II. Write a proper noun for each common noun below.

1. girl - _____   6. city - _____

2. cat - _____   7. movie - _____

3. teacher - _____   8. bike - _____

4. singer - _____   9. video game - _____

5. artist - _____   10. restaurant - _____

III. Write "Common" or "Proper" next to each noun.

1. FLOWER - _____   6. MT. WILSON - _____

2. DOCTOR - _____   7. STORE - _____

3. LINCOLN TUNNEL - _____ 8. COACH SMITH - _____

4. BEDROOM - _____   9. MARS - _____

5. BAMBI - _____   10. TRAINER - _____

Extension: Find a picture in a magazine. Make a list of all the proper nouns in the picture. Next, list ten (10) common nouns that you see.

Nouns
Definitions
#5

Singular and Plural Nouns

Singular Nouns name just one person, place, or thing.

Examples: girl, boy, dog, cat

The Trick: Draw a picture of one nun standing on first base. She just hit a single.

Plural Nouns name more than one person, place, or thing.

Examples: girls, boys, dogs, cats

The Trick: Plural sounds like squirrel. Draw a picture of a baseball field with a squirrel on each base. Remember that there are many squirrels on bases. They are the "plural squirrels".

Directions: Write "singular" or "plural" next to each noun.

1. nun - _____

2. squirrels - _____

3. rings - _____

4. toy - _____

5. people - _____

6. person - _____

7. car - _____

8. beds - _____

9. child - _____

10. children - _____

11. waiters - _____

12. ticket - _____

Nouns
Definitions
#6

I. Write the definitions for the nouns below. Remember the tricks.

Singular Nouns: _____

Plural Nouns: _____

II. Write "singular" or "plural" next to each noun.

1. trumpet - _____   11. flowers - _____

2. tacos - _____   12. geese - _____

3. baseball - _____   13. bottle - _____

4. bird - _____   14. mask - _____

5. flies - _____   15. players - _____

6. oxen - _____   16. cars - _____

7. house - _____   17. dream - _____

8. ships - _____   18. mice - _____

9. pilot - _____   19. dresses - _____

10. train - _____   20. shoe - _____

III. Look around the room. Make a list of five (5) singular nouns and five (5) plural nouns.

Singular	Plural
1. _____	1. _____
2. _____	2. _____
3. _____	3. _____
4. _____	4. _____
5. _____	5. _____

Nouns
Definitions
#7

I. Write the definitions for the nouns below. Remember the tricks.

Common Nouns: _____

Proper Nouns: _____

Singular Nouns: _____

Plural Nouns: _____

II. Write Person, Place, or Thing next to each word.

1. football - _____   5. field - _____

2. living room - _____   6. waiter - _____

3. quarterback - _____   7. love - _____

4. game - _____   8. park - _____

III. Write common or proper next to each noun. Next, tell whether the noun is singular or plural.

	Common / Proper	Singular / Plural
1. Mr. Jones	__Proper__	___singular___
2. teachers	_____	_____
3. pencils	_____	_____
4. Great Lakes	_____	_____
5. horse	_____	_____
6. balloons	_____	_____
7. Ryan	_____	_____
8. shoes	_____	_____
9. Statue of Liberty	_____	_____
10. cheerleader	_____	_____

Possessive Nouns

When a noun owns, or possesses, another item it is called a possessive noun.

Examples: John owns a book = John's book   The toys own a box = toys' box

Notice the apostrophe ('s) on John's book and the (s') on toys' box.

The apostrophe (') helps the noun show ownership.

Singular Nouns: Add ('s) to make the possessive. Rewrite the entire phrase below.

1. John_'s__ book

   ___**John's book**___

2. plane____ wing

   _____

3. bike____ wheel

   _____

4. door____ handle

   _____

5. Tom____ friend

   _____

6. room___ light

   _____

Directions: Write each possessive from above in a sentence. Draw an arrow from the possessive to the noun it possesses.

1. (John's book) - _____

2. (plane's wing) - _____

3. (bike's wheel) - _____

4. (door's handle) - _____

5. (Tom's friend) - _____

6. (room's light) - _____

Nouns
Possessive Nouns
#2

Plural Possessive Nouns

For singular nouns, the apostrophe (') and "s" have been added to the word.

Examples: toy's box   dog's bone   car's tires   girl's idea

For plural possessive nouns, the "s" is part of the word. Therefore, just add the apostrophe (').

Examples: several cats' owner   many crayons' box   players' coach

Plural Nouns: Just add (') to make the possessive. Rewrite the entire phrase below.

1. bees_'__ hive   2. friends____ parents   3. bikes____ wheels

__bees' hive___   _____   _____

4. planes____ wings   5. books____ covers   6. rooms___ lights

_____   _____   _____

Plural Nouns that do NOT end in "s": Add ('s) to make the possessive. Rewrite the
entire phrase below.

1. men_'s__ room   2. children____ toy   3. women____ club

__men's room___   _____   _____

4. deer____ meadow   5. geese____ pond   6. people___ houses

_____   _____   _____

Directions: Write each possessive below in a sentence. Draw an arrow from the
possessive to the noun it possesses.

1. (bees' hive) - _____

2. (children's toy) - _____

3. (bikes' wheels) - _____

4. (deer's meadow) - _____

5. (books' covers) - _____

6. (people's house) - _____

13

Name: _____

Possessive Noun Trick

"Possessive" is a tricky word. It simply means "to own". You have already learned that "noun" sounds like "nun". Therefore, draw a picture of a nun holding a book. Draw her holding the book tightly because it is HER book and she's very "possessive" of it.

Memorize:

The nun is very POSSESSIVE of her book.

Directions: Write the singular and plural possessives for each phrase below.

	Singular	Plural
1. bell of the cow	cow's bell	cows' bell
2. toy of the child		
3. bone of the dog		
4. sports of man		
5. thought of the king		
6. purse of the woman		
7. nest of the bird		
8. idea of the family		

Extension: Write any two (2) singular and any two (2) plural possessives from above in sentences.

Nouns
Possessive Nouns
#4

Write the definition of a possessive noun:

_____

I. Change each phrase below into a possessive.

1. The yard of Tim - ___**Tim's yard**___

2. Houses of the cities - _____

3. Cupboard of the dishes - _____

4. Animals of the farm - _____

5. Movie of the actors - _____

6. The play of the children - _____

7. The friend of Amy - _____

8. The price of the dresses - _____

II. Tell what each noun below owns. Be sure to add the ('s) or (').

1. book - ___**book's cover**___   6. chair - _____

2. horse - _____   7. parks - _____

3. dogs - _____   8. songs - _____

4. driver - _____   9. flower - _____

5. trees - _____   10. car - _____

III. Write any two (2) possessives from above in a sentence.

1._____

_____

2._____

_____

Nouns
Possessive Nouns
#5

Write the definition of a possessive noun:

_____

I. Change each phrase below into a possessive.

1. The purse of the lady - _____

2. The wool of the sheep - _____

3. Computers of the lab - _____

4. Ideas of several girls - _____

5. Crust of the bread - _____

6. The game of the students - _____

7. The puppy of the brothers - _____

8. The rider of the horse - _____

II. Tell what each noun below owns. Be sure to add the ('s) or (').

1. pencil - _____   6. team - _____

2. frogs - _____   7. fish - _____

3. countries - _____   8. men - _____

4. song - _____   9. bikes - _____

5. folders - _____   10. house - _____

III. Write any two (2) possessives from above in a sentence.

1._____

_____

2._____

_____

Nouns
Possessive Nouns
#6

I. Make a list of twelve (12) items that someone or something might own on a farm. Be creative.

Examples: pigs' trough   farmer's tractor

1. _____   7. _____

2. _____   8. _____

3. _____   9. _____

4. _____   10. _____

5. _____   11. _____

6. _____   12. _____

II. Write a story about an exciting day on a farm. Use at least six (6) possessives from your list above.

_____

_____

_____

_____

_____

_____

_____

_____

_____

_____

_____

_____

Nouns
Possessive Nouns
#7

I. Select a picture with a lot of action from a magazine or a poster. Write eight (8) possessives using the picture for ideas.

1. _____   5. _____

2. _____   6. _____

3. _____   7. _____

4. _____   8. _____

II. Write a story about the picture. Use the words from your list above.

_____

_____

_____

_____

_____

_____

_____

_____

_____

_____

_____

_____

_____

_____

_____

_____

_____

Noun Spelling

Rule

If a word ends in "y", preceded by a consonant, change the "y" to "i" and add "es".

country - countries	mystery - mysteries	spy - spies	cry - cries
hobby - hobbies	beauty - beauties	lady - ladies	try - tries
melody - melodies	injury - injuries	sky - skies	copy - copies
berry - berries	supply - supplies	fly - flies	

Rule #

If a word ends in "y", preceded by a vowel, just add "s" to make the word plural.

chimney - chimneys	turkey - turkeys	valley - valleys	birthday - birthdays
cowboy - cowboys			

Rule

If a word ends in "f" or "fe", the "f" or "fe" is usually changed to "v" and "es" is added to make the word plural. <u>Chief</u> and <u>belief</u> are two exceptions.

half - halves	thief - thieves	loaf - loaves	life - lives
wolf - wolves	leaf - leaves	self - selves	knife - knives
calf - calves	wife - wives	elf - elves	shelf - shelves

Rule

If a word ends in "o", just "s" is added to make the word plural.

piano - pianos	photo - photos	solo - solos	rodeo - rodeos
banjo - banjos	patio - patios	igloo - igloos	

* Sometimes exceptions are made plural by adding "es"

potato - potatoes	tomato - tomatoes	buffalo - buffaloes	tornado - tornadoes
hero - heroes			

Rule #

Some words form their plurals in unusual ways.

ox - oxen	foot - feet	tooth - teeth	mouse - mice
child - children	woman - women	goose - geese	deer - deer
sheep - sheep	man - men		

Rule

If a word ends in "ss", "x", "z", "sh", or "ch" the suffix "es" is usually added to make the word plural.

tax - taxes	branch - branches	glass - glasses	fox - foxes
church - churches	guess - guesses	waltz - waltzes	buzz - buzzes
punch - punches	flash - flashes	hunch - hunches	crutch - crutches
patch - patches	lunch - lunches	bunch - bunches	touch – touches

Rules #1 and #2

Rule #   If a word ends in "y", preceded by a consonant, change the "y" to "i" and add "es".

Examples: f<u>ly</u> = fl<u>ies</u>   cop<u>y</u> = cop<u>ies</u>

Directions: Rewrite the singular nouns as plurals.

1. try - _____

2. hobby - _____

3. spy - _____

4. country - _____

5. mystery - _____

6. beauty - _____

7. cry - _____

8. lady - _____

Rule # If a word ends in "y", preceded by a vowel, just add "s" to make the word plural.

Examples: tur<u>key</u> = tur<u>keys</u>   vall<u>ey</u> = vall<u>eys</u>

1. chimney - _____

2. birthday - _____

3. cowboy - _____

4. donkey- _____

5. key - _____

6. toy - _____

7. monkey- _____

8. bay- _____

Directions: Write four (4) sentences using any four (4) plural words from this page.

Example: It took three <u>tries</u> for Santa to climb down the <u>chimneys.</u>

1. _____

2. _____

3. _____

4. _____

Rules #1 and #2
Part 2

I. Write Rules #1 and #2 below and give two (2) examples of each:

Rule #1 - _____

    Example #1 _____   Example #2 _____

Rule #2 - _____

    Example #1 _____   Example #2 _____

II. Rewrite the singular nouns as plurals. Write the number of the rule next to each word.

Rule #   **Rule #**

__1__   1. melody - __**melodies**__   _____ 11. birthday- _____

_____   2. cowboy - _____   _____ 12. injury - _____

_____   3. sky - _____   _____ 13. monkey- _____

_____   4. copy - _____   _____ 14. berry - _____

_____   5. chimney - _____   _____ 15. supply - _____

_____   6. donkey - _____   _____ 16. bay - _____

_____   7. fly - _____   _____ 17. mystery - _____

_____   8. toy - _____   _____ 18. spy - _____

_____   9. country - _____   _____ 19. key - _____

_____   10. hobby - _____   _____ 20. lady - _____

Directions: Write four (4) sentences using two (2) plural words in the same sentence. Use one plural word from Rule #1 and one plural word from Rule #2.

    Example: It took three <u>tries</u> for Santa to climb down the <u>chimneys.</u>

1. _____

2. _____

3. _____

4. _____

Rules #1 and #2
Part 3

I. Write the **plural** forms of the words below in a sentence.

1. (hobby / birthday) _____

_____

2. (fly / berry) _____

_____

3. (mystery / turkey) _____

_____

4. (lady / chimney) _____

_____

5. (supply / valley) _____

_____

II. Write the **plural** forms of the words below three times.

1. country - _____

2. injury - _____

3. cowboy - _____

4. spy - _____

5. bay - _____

6. copy - _____

7. beauty - _____

8. melody - _____

Rules #1 and #2
Quiz

1. hobby - _____

2. turkey - _____

3. berry - _____

4. fly - _____

5. birthday - _____

6. cowboy - _____

7. injury - _____

8. copy - _____

9. chimney - _____

10. valley - _____

11. cry - _____

12. country - _____

13. mystery - _____

14. melody - _____

15. supply - _____

16. donkey - _____

17. spy - _____

18. lady - _____

19. toy - _____

20. beauty - _____

21. sky - _____

22. try - _____

Rules #3 and #4
PLURALS

Rule # 3   If a word ends in "f" or "fe", the "f" or "fe" is usually changed to "v", and "es" is added to make the word plural. <u>Chief</u> and <u>belief</u> are two exceptions.

Examples: hal<u>f</u> = hal<u>ves</u>   kni<u>fe</u> = kni<u>ves</u>

Directions: Rewrite the singular nouns as plurals.

1. wolf - _____
2. wife - _____
3. *belief - _____
4. thief - _____
5. self - _____

6. calf - _____
7. *chief - _____
8. life - _____
9. elf - _____
10. shelf - _____

Rule # 4   If a word ends in "o", just "s" is added to make the word plural. * Sometimes exceptions are made plural by adding "es": potato / tomato / buffalo / tornado / hero

1. banjo - _____
2. potato - _____
3. igloo - _____
4. rodeo - _____
5. tornado - _____

6. buffalo - _____
7. tomato - _____
8. solo - _____
9. hero - _____
10. patio - _____

Directions: Write four (4) sentences using two (2) plural words in the same sentence. Use one plural word from Rule #3 and one plural word from Rule #4.

Example: Three <u>wolves</u> chased the <u>buffaloes</u>.

1. _____
2. _____
3. _____
4. _____

Rules #3 and #4
Part 2

I. Write Rules #3 and #4 below and give two (2) examples:

Rule #3 - _____

Example #1 _____ Example #2 _____

Rule #4 - _____

Example #1 _____ Example #2 _____

II. Rewrite the singular nouns as plurals. Write the number of the rule next to each word.

Rule #   **Rule #**

__3__ 1. leaf - __**leaves**__   _____ 11. rodeo - _____

_____ 2. hero - _____   _____ 12. thief - _____

_____ 3. wolf - _____   _____ 13. solo - _____

_____ 4. patio - _____   _____ 14. tornado - _____

_____ 5. buffalo - _____   _____ 15. loaf - _____

_____ 6. knife - _____   _____ 16. life - _____

_____ 7. self - _____   _____ 17. photo - _____

_____ 8. banjo - _____   _____ 18. potato - _____

_____ 9. tomato - _____   _____ 19. shelf - _____

_____ 10. half - _____   _____ 20. piano - _____

Directions: Write four (4) sentences using one plural word from Rules #3 and #4.

Example: The <u>wives</u> took many <u>photos</u> of the children.

1. _____

2. _____

3. _____

4. _____

Rules #3 and #4
Part 3

I. Write the **plural** forms of the words below in a sentence.

   1. (thief / piano) _____

   _____

   2. (elf / igloo) _____

   _____

   3. (knife / potato) _____

   _____

   4. (shelf / photo) _____

   _____

   5. (hero / tornado) _____

   _____

II. Write the **plural** forms of the words below three times.

   1. half - _____

   2. banjo - _____

   3. wolf - _____

   4. tomato - _____

   5. patio - _____

   6. wife - _____

   7. solo - _____

   8. rodeo - _____

Rules #3 and #4
Quiz

1. calf - _____

2. piano - _____

3. potato - _____

4. wife - _____

5. loaf - _____

6. rodeo - _____

7. wolf - _____

8. thief - _____

9. patio - _____

10. self - _____

11. hero - _____

12. life - _____

13. tornado - _____

14. half - _____

15. banjo - _____

16. leaf - _____

17. igloo - _____

18. buffalo - _____

19. elf - _____

20. tomato - _____

21. shelf - _____

22. photo - _____

23. knife - _____

24. solo - _____

Rules #5 and #6

PLURALS

Rule # 5   Some words form their plurals in unusual ways.

ox - oxen	foot - feet	tooth - teeth	mouse - mice
child - children	woman - women	goose - geese	deer - deer
sheep - sheep	man - men		

Rule # 6   If a word ends in "ss", "x", "z", "sh", or "ch" the suffix "es" is usually added to make the word plural.

tax - taxes	branch - branches	glass - glasses	fox - foxes
church - churches	guess - guesses	waltz - waltzes	buzz - buzzes
punch - punches	flash - flashes	hunch - hunches	crutch - crutches
patch - patches	lunch - lunches	bunch - bunches	touch – touches

Directions: Rewrite the singular nouns as plurals.

1. goose - _____   8. sheep - _____

2. church - _____   9. lunch - _____

3. branch - _____   10. child - _____

4. deer - _____   11. tooth - _____

5. guess - _____   12. glass - _____

6. ox - _____   13. crutch - _____

7. fox - _____   14. mouse - _____

Directions: Write four (4) sentences using two (2) plural words in the same sentence. Use one plural word from Rule #5 and one plural word from Rule #6.

Example: The <u>women</u> danced <u>waltzes</u> with the men.

1. _____

2. _____

3. _____

4. _____

Rules #5 and #6
Part 2

I. Write Rules #5 and #6 below and give two (2) examples:

Rule #5 - _____

Example #1 _____   Example #2 _____

Rule #6 - _____

Example #1 _____   Example #2 _____

II. Rewrite the singular nouns as plurals. Write the number of the rule next to each word.

Rule #

Rule #

_5_ 1. sheep - __**sheep**__   _____ 11. tooth - _____

_____ 2. patch - _____   _____ 12. deer - _____

_____ 3. man - _____   _____ 13. church - _____

_____ 4. flash - _____   _____ 14. woman - _____

_____ 5. ox - _____   _____ 15. branch - _____

_____ 6. punch - _____   _____ 16. goose - _____

_____ 7. guess - _____   _____ 17. glass - _____

_____ 8. child - _____   _____ 18. foot - _____

_____ 9. lunch - _____   _____ 19. tax - _____

_____ 10. fox - _____   _____ 20. mouse - _____

Directions: Write four (4) sentences using two (2) plural words in the same sentence. Use one plural word from Rule #5 and one plural word from Rule #6.

Example: The <u>women</u> made <u>lunches</u> for the children.

1. _____

2. _____

3. _____

4. _____

Rules #5 and #6
Part 3

I. Write the **plural** forms of the words below in a sentence.

1. (ox / patch) _____

    _____

2. (goose / bunch) _____

    _____

3. (flash / deer) _____

    _____

4. (buzz / mouse) _____

    _____

5. (man / guess) _____

    _____

II. Write the **plural** forms of the words below three times.

1. sheep - _____

2. punch - _____

3. foot - _____

4. tax - _____

5. tooth - _____

6. waltz - _____

7. child - _____

8. branch - _____

Rules #5 and #6
Quiz

1. tax - _____

2. woman - _____

3. crutch - _____

4. punch - _____

5. touch - _____

6. mouse - _____

7. foot - _____

8. buzz - _____

9. deer - _____

10. lunch - _____

11. glass - _____

12. patch - _____

13. tooth - _____

14. guess - _____

15. ox - _____

16. sheep - _____

17. waltz - _____

18. fox - _____

19. hunch - _____

20. man - _____

21. bunch - _____

22. goose - _____

23. flash - _____

24. church - _____

25. child - _____

26. branch - _____

Noun Review
#1

I. Write the definitions of the following nouns:

Common Noun: _____

Proper Noun: _____

Singular Noun: _____

Plural Noun: _____

Possessive Noun: _____

II. Put an "x" below each word that fits the noun on the left.

	Singular	Plural	Common	Proper	Possessive
1. doctor's	X	____	X	____	X
2. Jeff	____	____	____	____	____
3. cows	____	____	____	____	____
4. New York's	____	____	____	____	____
5. flower	____	____	____	____	____
6. rocks	____	____	____	____	____
7. brothers'	____	____	____	____	____
8. road	____	____	____	____	____
9. Arizona's	____	____	____	____	____
10. Ms. Daisy	____	____	____	____	____
11. clowns	____	____	____	____	____
12. baskets	____	____	____	____	____
13. hammers'	____	____	____	____	____
14. sun	____	____	____	____	____
15. Anna's	____	____	____	____	____

Noun Review
#2

I. Put an "x" below each word that fits the noun on the left.

	Singular	Plural	Common	Proper	Possessive
1. Mt. Hood	_____	_____	_____	_____	_____
2. Mike's	_____	_____	_____	_____	_____
3. spoons	_____	_____	_____	_____	_____
4. children's	_____	_____	_____	_____	_____
5. Great Lakes	_____	_____	_____	_____	_____
6. ducks'	_____	_____	_____	_____	_____
7. game	_____	_____	_____	_____	_____
8. Play Station	_____	_____	_____	_____	_____
9. teachers'	_____	_____	_____	_____	_____
10. cities	_____	_____	_____	_____	_____

II. **Possessive Nouns:** Change each phrase below into a possessive.

1. cabin of the neighbor - _____

2. flower of the desert - _____

3. author of the stories - _____

4. animals of the farm - _____

5. movie of the actors - _____

6. feelings of your friends - _____

III. **Plural Noun Spelling Rules:**
Directions: Change these singular nouns into plural nouns.

1. city - _____   4. toy - _____   7. fly - _____

2. church - _____   5. life - _____   8. monkey - _____

3. solo - _____   6. guess - _____   9. self - _____

Unit 2

Capitalization

Proper Nouns

Geographical Names

Historical Periods

Holidays

Special Events

_____
Student

Capitalization

	Mastery	Non-Mastery
1. Proper and Common Nouns		
2. Geographical Names		
3. Historical Periods		
4. Holidays		
5. Special Events		

Capitalization
Common and Proper Nouns
#1

Common Nouns: A common noun names any person, place or thing. Common nouns are <u>not</u> capitalized.

Person: girl   *Place: park*   *Thing: apple*

Proper Nouns: A proper noun names an exact person, place, or thing. Proper nouns <u>are</u> capitalized.

Person: Sally   *Place: Bloomfield Park*   *Thing: Kleenex*

Warning: Some words can be confusing. For example, "apple" is the specific name of a fruit, but is it a proper noun? Because there are many apples in the world, "apple" is not a proper noun. If we gave the apple a name–Bob, for example–Bob would be the specific name of the apple. Thus, Bob would be capitalized.

The Trick: Because common nouns name any person, place, or thing, you can usually put a or the in front of a common noun. Therefore, if you want to know whether a noun is common or proper noun, try putting "a" or "the" in front of it. If you can, it is probably a common noun. If you can't, it is probably a proper noun.

I. **Directions:** Write "Proper" or "Common" on the line. Next, rewrite the word. Capitalize the first letter if it is a proper noun. Finally, write "Person", "Place", or "Thing" on the next line.

Common or Proper?		Rewrite Word	Person, Place, or Thing?
___Common___	1. DOG	___dog___	___thing___
_____	2. MT. WILSON	_____	_____
_____	3. STREET	_____	_____
_____	4. BEAVER	_____	_____
_____	5. TEXAS	_____	_____
_____	6. SNAKE RIVER	_____	_____
_____	7. ISLAND	_____	_____
_____	8. BANANA	_____	_____
_____	9. TEACHER	_____	_____
_____	10. MR. DEAN	_____	_____

Capitalization
Common and Proper Nouns
#2

Directions: Write "Proper" or "Common" on the left line. Next, rewrite the word.
Capitalize the first letter if it is a proper noun. Finally, write "Person," "Place," or "Thing"
on the next line.

Proper / Common Noun		Rewrite Word	Person, Place, or Thing
_____	1. HOME	_____	_____
_____	2. PACIFIC OCEAN	_____	_____
_____	3. DR. DREW	_____	_____
_____	4. PIZZA	_____	_____
_____	5. BANK	_____	_____
_____	6. CIRCUS	_____	_____
_____	7. OLYMPICS	_____	_____
_____	8. PRINCIPAL	_____	_____
_____	9. MARS	_____	_____
_____	10. PENCIL	_____	_____
_____	11. MEXICO	_____	_____
_____	12. CLOCK	_____	_____

Extension: Where did your friends go? Write five (5) sentences about
people you know. Tell the exact place where they went.

Example: Yesterday, Donna went to Downey.

Capitalization
Common and Proper Nouns
#3

Geographical Names: One type of proper noun is a geographical name.
This is the <u>exact name</u> of any place.

Examples: *Lake Tahoe   Big Bear   Grand Canyon   Hawaii*

Historical Periods: One type of proper noun is a historical period.
This is the <u>exact name</u> of any period of time.

Examples: *Middle Ages   Stone Age   Mesozoic Era*

Directions: Write **C** if the noun is a common noun; write **P** if the noun is a proper noun. If the proper noun is a geographical name, circle "GN". If the proper noun is a historical period, circle "HP".

__C__ LAKE	GN HP	_____ PLANET	GN HP
__P__ LAKE TAHOE		_____ PLUTO	
_____ CITY	GN HP	_____ RENAISSANCE	GN HP
_____ BELLFLOWER		_____ DECADE	
_____ JURASSIC PERIOD	GN HP	_____ YOSEMITE	GN HP
_____ YEAR		_____ PARK	
_____ SACRAMENTO	GN HP	_____ MEXICO	GN HP
_____ CAPITAL		_____ COUNTRY	
_____ SPRING	GN HP	_____ AGE OF EXPLORATION	
_____ IMPRESSIONIST PERIOD		_____ CENTURY	GN HP

Extension: Write (5) five geographical locations (places) that are common nouns and five (5) that are proper nouns. Write them on a separate sheet of paper.

Example: park – Central Park

Capitalization
Common and Proper Nouns
#4

Holidays: Other types of proper nouns are holidays.
These are exact names of special days.

Examples: *Labor Day   Arbor Day   Christmas   Easter*

Special Events: Other types of proper nouns are special events.

Examples: *Miss America Pageant   Thanksgiving Day Parade*

Directions: Rewrite the words below. Be sure to capitalize the important letters. Next, if it is a holiday, circle "holiday." If it is a special event, circle "special event."

1. independence day - _____   Holiday   Special Event

2. lindstrom's talent show - _____   Holiday   Special Event

3. arbor day - _____   Holiday   Special Event

4. rose parade - _____   Holiday   Special Event

5. valentine's day - _____   Holiday   Special Event

6. beth temple bake sale - _____   Holiday   Special Event

7. memorial day - _____   Holiday   Special Event

8. thanksgiving - _____   Holiday   Special Event

9. opening day- _____   Holiday   Special Event

10. labor day - _____   Holiday   Special Event

11. kentucky derby - _____   Holiday   Special Event

12. christmas - _____   Holiday   Special Event

13. olympics - _____   Holiday   Special Event

14. lakewood's firework spectacular - _____

Holiday   Special Event

Extension: Select any five (5) holidays or special events from above. Write them in a sentence on a separate sheet of paper.

Capitalization
Common and Proper Nouns
#5

I. Circle the P if the noun is proper. Circle C if the noun is common. Next, rewrite the word on the line. If it is a proper noun, be sure to capitalize the first letter.

P   C   1. CENTRAL VALLEY - _____

P   C   2. BIRTHDAY - _____

P   C   3. ST. PATRICK'S DAY - _____

P   C   4. SPACE - _____

P   C   5. HANUKKAH - _____

P   C   6. SODA - _____

P   C   7. SNAKE RIVER - _____

P   C   8. MOUNTAIN - _____

P   C   9. IRON AGE - _____

P   C   10. BLACK HISTORY MONTH - _____

P   C   11. SPACE SHUTTLE - _____

P   C   12. OPENING DAY - _____

P   C   13. PARTY - _____

P   C   14. HALLOWEEN - _____

II. Write any four (4) proper nouns from above in a sentence.

1. _____

2. _____

3. _____

4. _____

Capitalization
Common and Proper Nouns
#6

Name: _____

I. Circle the P if the noun is proper. Circle C if the noun is common. Next, rewrite the word on the line. If it is a proper noun, be sure to capitalize the first letter.

P   C   1. NEW YORK - _____

P   C   2. FIRST COMMUNION - _____

P   C   3. PARADE - _____

P   C   4. ICE AGE - _____

P   C   5. NEW YEAR'S EVE - _____

P   C   6. MIDNIGHT - _____

P   C   7. CALIFORNIA - _____

P   C   8. RIVER - _____

P   C   9. EASTER - _____

P   C   10. THANKSGIVING - _____

II. Write two examples of each rule on the lines below. Use the list of words from above.

Geographical Names

1. _____   2. _____

Holidays

1. _____   2. _____

Special Events

1. _____   2. _____

Extension: Write any four (4) proper nouns from Part II in a sentence.

Capitalization
Common and Proper Nouns
#7

I. **Directions**: Write Proper or Common on the line.   Rewrite the word with the proper punctuation below the word.

_____Proper_____	1. GRAND CANYON	_____	9. ROGET'S DICTIONARY
Grand Canyon			
_____	2. RIVER	_____	10. KICKBALL
_____	3. MOON	_____	11. GRAND CANYON
_____	4. STATE	_____	12. FLORIDA
_____	5. PIZZA HUT	_____	13. ORANGE JUICE
_____	6. JUPITER	_____	14. CAKE
_____	7. MOUNTAIN	_____	15. WORLD WAR II
_____	8. JIMMY	_____	16. EGG

II. Directions: In the story below, circle all the common nouns. Cross out all the proper nouns and rewrite them with the correct punctuation below.

~~mom~~ and ~~dad~~ gave me an incredible (surprise) for my birthday last week. I crawled out
Mom   **Dad**
of bed that morning and expected to find a mountain of presents on our dinning room table.

Instead, my mom said, "Get dressed. We're going somewhere." My heart pounded as I wondered

where we could be going.   The renaissance fair? The bugs bunny film festival? The empire state

building? The movies?

As my dad's chevy suburban pulled onto the golden state freeway, I thought I was going to die

with excitement. Before I knew it we were pulling off the freeway, and I could see the white mountain

of the matterhorn, a cool ride, rising into the sky. It was disneyland!

When we arrived at the park, many of my friends were there with presents in their hands and big

smiles on their faces. There was randy, helen, michael, lisa, and my cousin, skeeter. Everyone was

dressed in wonderful medieval period costumes. What a great surprise. After going on rides all day like

space mountain, big thunder mountain, and the haunted mansion, it was time to go home. What a great

birthday!

Capitalization
Common and Proper Nouns
#8

Directions: In the story below, cross out all the proper nouns, and rewrite them with the correct punctuation in the space below.

In the old west there's a story about a boy named the licorice kid. He may have been only ten years old, but he was the roughest, toughest, meanest hombre to walk the small desert towns of new mexico. Nobody knows where he came from, but many people say he just appeared one day out of a dusty wind coming down from texas. Riding on his trusty steed, buttercup, the licorice kid roams the vast fields of albuquerque rescuing strangers in need.

He earned his nickname one dry, hot day when the town bully, pokemon pete, returned from ballet camp. Pokemon pete immediately rounded up all the kids in the neighborhood and started forcing them to do ballet moves between the rolling tumbleweeds at sunflower park. Suddenly, there was the crack of a whip. It was the licorice kid, and he didn't look happy.

Pokemon pete, his braces gleaming in the blazing sun, squinted at the kid daring him to make his move. The kid squinted back and ripped a bite off his long red licorice whip. As the two slowly and deliberately marched their way toward each other, the tension was just too much to bear. A baby started to cry, jose hid behind his lemonade stand, and little girls clutched their tickle-me-elmo dolls to their chest.

The two stood facing each other, their arms arched by the sides of their levis, for what seemed like an eternity. No one moved a muscle. Wind whistled through the park and an eagle screeched overhead. Suddenly, pokemon pete made his move.

"I'll trade you a charizar for a piece of that licorice," he said with a deep, raspy voice.

"Sure," whispered the kid.

From that day on, pokemon pete was a new man. No more bullying. He traded his pokemon cards to get what he wanted.

Whatever happened to the licorice kid? No one knows for sure. Some say he rode a wells fargo wagon to california, offering licorice to gold miners near sacramento. But here in albuquerque, he'll always be in our hearts.

Extension: How many common nouns can you find in this story? Circle as many as you can find.

Capitalization
Common and Proper Nouns
Test Review

Directions: Write Proper or Common on the left line. Next, rewrite the word. Capitalize the first letter if it is a proper noun. Finally, write "Person," "Place," or "Thing" on the next line.

Proper / Common Noun		Rewrite Word	Person, Place, or Thing
_____	1. CALIFORNIA **GN**	_____	_____
_____	2. PACIFIC OCEAN	_____	_____
_____	3. DOCTOR	_____	_____
_____	4. WORLD WAR II	_____	_____
_____	5. CITY	_____	_____
_____	6. SAN DIEGO	_____	_____
_____	7. PENCIL	_____	_____
_____	8. BLACK HISTORY MONTH	_____	_____
_____	9. MISS AMERICA PAGEANT	_____	_____
_____	10. ALLIGATOR	_____	_____
_____	11. COMPUTER	_____	_____
_____	12. NEW YEAR'S EVE	_____	_____
_____	13. BRIDGE	_____	_____
_____	14. CAMERA	_____	_____
_____	15. KENTUCKY DERBY	_____	_____

Extra Credit: For each <u>proper noun</u>, explain whether it is a **Geographical Name(GN), Historical Period(HP), Holiday (H), or Special Event(SE).** Write GN, HP, Holiday, or SE next to each proper noun from above.

Unit 3

Pronouns

Verbs: Past, Present, and Future

Adjectives

Contractions

_____
Student

Parts of Speech

	Mastery	Non-Mastery
1. Pronouns		
2. Verbs: Past, Present, and Future		
3. Adjectives		
4. Contractions		

Parts of Speech - Ch. 3
Study Sheet

Directions: Use this sheet to practice the parts of speech in this chapter. Fill it out as you study each part of speech.

Pronouns Pronouns take the place of a _____.

```
┌─────────────────────────────┐
│                             │
│                             │
│                             │
│                             │
│                             │
│                             │
│        Study Picture        │
└─────────────────────────────┘
```

Examples: John = __he__ or _____

people = _____ or __**them**__

Tina's = _____

Verbs The three kinds of verbs are:

1. _____

Examples: _____

2. _____

Examples: _____

3. _____

Examples: _____

```
┌─────────────────────────────┐
│                             │
│                             │
│                             │
│                             │
│                             │
│        Study Picture        │
└─────────────────────────────┘
```

Adjectives Adjectives describe a _____ or a _____.

```
┌─────────────────────────────┐
│                             │
│                             │
│                             │
│                             │
│        Study Picture        │
└─────────────────────────────┘
```

Adjectives answer the questions:

1. _____

Examples: _____

2. _____

Examples: _____

3. _____

Examples: _____

Pronouns
#1

Pronouns A pronoun takes the place of a noun.

Examples: John = <u>he</u> or <u>him</u>

people = <u>they</u> or <u>them</u>

Tina's = <u>her</u> or <u>hers</u>

The Trick:
You already know that "noun" sounds like "nun". When you think of a pronoun, think of a "professional nun". Draw a nun with a hat that says "Pro". Draw another nun walking away because she's being replaced by a "professional nun".

Study Picture

What's wrong with the story below?

John was invited to Tina's birthday party. John wanted to get Tina a good present. However, John wasn't sure what to get Tina. Tina really likes stuffed animals, but John wasn't sure which one Tina would like. So John thought and John thought. Suddenly, John got a great idea. John would get Tina a gift certificate so Tina could select a bear Tina would really like. John was now very excited about Tina's birthday party.

1. Circle every "John", "Tina", and "Tina's" in the story above.
2. How many times is the word "John" used? _____ Circle all of the John's.
3. How many times is the word "Tina" or Tina's" used? _____

Extension: Rewrite the story from above. Keep the topic sentence. Next, replace John, Tina, and Tina's with the pronouns:

he, him, his, she, her, hers

Pronouns
#2

Name: _____

Subject Pronouns						
I	you	he	she	we	they	it
Object Pronouns						
me	you	him	her	us	them	it
Possessive Pronouns						
my	mine	your(s)	his	her(s)	our(s)	their(s)	its

Directions: Write all of the pronouns that can replace the nouns below. If you see (Your name: _____), write your name on the line.

1. Mr. Saito - _____

2. Rachel and Molly - _____

3. Candice - _____

4. our class - _____

5. (Your name: _____) - _____

6. pencil - _____

7. Tammy and (Your name: _____) - _____

8. football players - _____

9. book - _____

10. coaches - _____

11. Mrs. Morrison - _____

12. you and your best friend - _____

Pronouns
#3

Write the definition of a pronoun:

_____

Directions: Rewrite the sentences by changing the underlined nouns to pronouns.

1. <u>Lupe</u> gave a <u>present</u> to <u>Gena</u>.

   _____**She** gave **it** to **her**._____

2. The <u>dog</u> chased the <u>cats</u>.

   _____

3. <u>Nurses</u> give <u>medicine</u> to <u>patients</u>.

   _____

4. <u>Mom</u> baked <u>cookies</u> for <u>Tina and me</u>.

   _____

5. <u>Ron and I</u> snuck some <u>candy</u> into the <u>theater</u>.

   _____

6. <u>Dave</u> sent <u>Wilma and Betty's</u> clothes to <u>Mrs. Smith</u>.

   _____

7. <u>Coach Smith</u> made <u>the team</u> run laps around the <u>field</u>.

   _____

8. <u>Hillary and Bill</u> traveled with <u>Chelsea</u> to <u>George's</u> ranch.

   _____

Extension: Write the pronouns below in a story about someone grocery shopping. Remember, do NOT use a pronoun until you have stated the noun first.

she   her   it   them   our

Pronouns
#4

Write the definition of a pronoun:

_____

Directions: Rewrite the sentences by changing the nouns to pronouns.

1. <u>Dad</u> built <u>the bike</u> for <u>my brother</u>, and <u>my brother</u> really liked <u>the bike</u>.

   _____

2. <u>Ralph and I</u> read <u>the book</u> to <u>our class</u>.

   _____

3. <u>Gina and Linda's</u> grades were better than <u>Cindy's</u> grades.

   _____

4. The <u>mail carrier</u> sent a <u>letter</u> to <u>Bob</u> by mistake.

   _____

5. Making <u>Mike and Dawn</u> sing <u>a song</u> is like making a <u>pig</u> fly.

   _____

6. <u>Donna's</u> joke made <u>Vince and Tommy</u> laugh so they retold <u>the joke</u>.

   _____

7. This is <u>Greg's</u> book so put <u>the book</u> where <u>Greg</u> can find <u>the book</u>.

   _____

8. <u>My friends</u> let <u>Heather and Sally</u> join <u>the club</u>.

   _____

9. <u>The television</u> showed <u>dolphins</u> bouncing <u>a ball</u> on the <u>dolphin's</u> noses.

   _____

10. <u>The Dodgers</u> play <u>the Angels</u>, but <u>Tom and I</u> can't see <u>the game</u>.

    _____

Pronouns
#5

Directions: Fill in the blanks with a pronoun that fits.

1. __They__ gave all __their__ homework to __him__ .

2. _____ like to play with _____ .

3. _____ chewed a hole in _____ sock so I had to replace _____ .

4. _____ played with _____ for an hour until _____ had to go home.

5. _____ cat likes to be scratched behind _____ ears.

6. _____ used _____ strong muscles to lift _____ over the fence.

7. _____ wrote _____ a letter and mailed _____ that night.

8. _____ didn't know that the toy was _____ so we gave it away.

9. _____ game needs batteries so I bought _____ at the store.

10. Coach told _____ that if _____ play hard then _____ would win.

11. _____ whistle was loud, and it hurt _____ ears.

12. _____ invited _____ to _____ party.

Extension: Write the possessive pronouns below in a story about a birthday party for you. Remember, do NOT use a pronoun until you have stated the noun first.

my   her   its   their

Pronouns
#6

I. Directions: Circle all of the pronouns in the story below. Can you find all 31?

The children had a great time at camp. First, they got off the bus and found their cabin. It was very nice. Then, the counselor said, "I want you to put your clothes on hangers then put them in the closet." He then gave them a ticket to get lunch. Later, the teacher took her students on a nature walk. When they returned, the staff showed them how to make crafts. One student asked the head counselor, " Can we take them home with us?" He said that we could take them home and show them to our parents. When the trip was over, the campers packed their suitcases. Amy couldn't find her craft until she was finished packing. It was in her friend's suitcase who knew it wasn't hers. Amy was happy to find it and show it to her mom when she got home.

II. When a writer uses many pronouns, it may be hard to understand the noun that the pronoun is replacing. The noun being replaced is called the **antecedent**. In the story above, draw an arrow from each pronoun to its antecedent. Feel free to use different colored crayons or colored pencils. It's going to get messy ☺ .

Example:

The children had a great time at camp. First, they got off the bus and found their cabin.

Extension: Write a story about someone playing a game. Use the five (5) pronouns below. When finished, circle your pronouns and draw an arrow to the antecedent. If each pronoun does not have a written antecedent, you need to fix your story so that it does have an antecedent.

| **He** | **their** | **my** | **her** | **our** |

Verbs
#1

Here are three kinds of verbs:

1. Action Words   -   run, jump, play, love, wish

2. "To Be" Verbs   -   is, are, was, were, be

3. Helping verbs   -   <u>is</u> running, <u>are</u> jumping, <u>was</u> playing

The Trick: The word "verb" starts with the letter V. Make a V with your fingers. Turn it upside down and make an " with the finger on your other hand. The A stands for Action! * As you do this, say to yourself, "A verb," (Make the V) "is an action word." (Make the A)

I. How many action verbs can you think of that start with the letters below. Write at least five (5) for each letter.

C	P	S	T
__cut__	_____	_____	_____
_____	_____	_____	_____
_____	_____	_____	_____
_____	_____	_____	_____
_____	_____	_____	_____

II. Circle the verbs in each sentence below.

1. Amy gave me a cookie.

2. Run to the store for some milk.

3. I want an ice cream.

4. The students behind me waited for three hours.

5. She was happy so she brought me some flowers.

6. We are camping at the park.

Verbs
#2

A verb shows _____

      Examples: sing, run, jump

I. How many action verbs can you write that start with the letters below.
  Write at least five (5) for each letter.

A	R	M	G
_____	_____	_____	_____
_____	_____	_____	_____
_____	_____	_____	_____
_____	_____	_____	_____
_____	_____	_____	_____

II. Fill in the blank with a verb that fits the sentence.

1. The teacher _____ the students a test.

2. She _____ all of the cookies.

3. He will _____ in the first race and _____ the second race.

4. I _____ for my sister after school so I can _____ home with her.

5. I _____ a letter to my friend, and my mom _____ it.

6. Grandpa said he would _____ me a dollar if I _____ a song.

7. Tanya _____ eating some watermelon under the tree.

8. They _____ excited about their chance to _____ to Disneyland.

9. Airplanes _____ over our house every day.

10. In baseball it is important to _____ the ball and _____ quickly.

Extension: Write any five (5) verbs from Part I in a sentence.

Verbs
#3

Name: _____

Verbs are action words. We can use them to talk about action that has taken place in the past, action that is taking place now, or action that will be taking place in the future. As a result, verbs have a past, present and future **tense**.

Past Tense	Present Tense	Future Tense
talked	talk	will talk
ran	run	will run

I. Write the past, present, and future tense for the words below.

	Past Tense	Present Tense	Future Tense
1. talk -	_____	_____	_____
2. walked -	_____	_____	_____
3. know -	_____	_____	_____
4. will look -	_____	_____	_____
5. spoke -	_____	_____	_____
6. arrive -	_____	_____	_____
7. sit -	_____	_____	_____
8. will teach -	_____	_____	_____

II. Write "past," "present," or "future" depending on the tense of the verb.

1. play - _____

   will play - _____

   played - _____

2. sang - _____

   sing - _____

   will sing - _____

3. climb - _____

   will climb - _____

   climbed - _____

4. ate - _____

    eat - _____

    will eat - _____

5. jump - _____

    will jump - _____

    jumped - _____

6. will swim - _____

    swam - _____

    swim - _____

Verbs
#4

I. Write the past, present, and future tense for the words below.

	Past Tense	Present Tense	Future Tense
1. sing -	_____	_____	_____
2. thought -	_____	_____	_____
3. love -	_____	_____	_____
4. will type -	_____	_____	_____
5. fight -	_____	_____	_____
6. left -	_____	_____	_____
7. hit -	_____	_____	_____
8. will sail -	_____	_____	_____

II. Write "past," "present," or "future" depending on the tense of the verb.

1. fly - _____

   will fly - _____

2. danced - _____

   dance - _____

3. wish - _____

   will wish - _____

4. go - _____

   went - _____

5. hurried - _____

   will hurry - _____

6. will borrow - _____

   borrowed - _____

Extension: A common mistake for young writers is to mix the tenses in a story. Sometimes they start writing the story as if something is currently happening. Then they switch in the middle of the story and start writing as if something has already happened.

Write a three (3) sentence story (one paragraph maximum) about something that happened to you earlier in the week. Next, rewrite the story as if it is happening to you right now. Finally, rewrite the story a third time. Pretend that you are predicting what will happen to you some time in the future.

Verbs
#5

When is a verb not an action word? When the verb is "being". Here are five (5) words that show action by saying that something is just "being".

is   are   was   were   am

Examples:

He **is** happy.   They **are** happy.

She **was** happy.   We **were** happy.

I **am** happy.

Directions: Fill in the blanks with the correct "being" verb.

is   are   was   were   am

1. I _____ a good student.

2. We _____ sad about the sick child.

3. _____ they hungry for more pizza?

4. He _____ our class president.

5. Tina and Amy _____ cheerleaders.

6. Last week he _____ angry about the accident.

7. _____ I in trouble?

8. Yesterday, he _____ late for school.

9. The puppy _____ lonely when we went to school.

10. _____ the teacher ready to teach?

Extension: Write five (5) sentences using the "to be" verbs:

is are was were am

Verbs
#6

I. List five (5) action verbs and five (5) "to be" verbs:

Action Verbs: _____ _____ _____ _____ _____

"To-Be" Verbs: _____ _____ _____ _____ _____

Helping Verbs: Helping verbs help the main verb give a more accurate meaning.

Verb Phrase: The helping verb(s) join the main verb to make a verb phrase.

Examples:

Helping Verb(s)	**+**	**Main Verb**	**=**	**Verb Phrase**
is		playing		is playing
should have		waited		should have waited
would have been		late		would have been late

Helping Verbs
is   are   was   were   am
be   been   being   can   could   did   do
does   had   has   have   may   might
must   shall   should   will   would

Directions: List three verb phrases for each action verb below. Use the helping verbs in the box above.

1. play - __can play__ , __does play__ , __will play__

2. working - _____ , _____ , _____

3. stopped - _____ , _____ , _____

4. smell - _____ , _____ , _____

5. written - _____ , _____ , _____

6. laughing - _____ , _____ , _____

61

Verbs
#7

I. Directions: List three verb phrases for each action verb below. Use the helping verbs from Verbs #6 for ideas.

1. sing - __could sing__ , __must sing__ , __would sing__

2. crying - _____ , _____ , _____

3. shopped - _____ , _____ , _____

4. sung - _____ , _____ , _____

5. fight - _____ , _____ , _____

6. helped - _____ , _____ , _____

7. typing - _____ , _____ , _____

8. baked - _____ , _____ , _____

II. "To Be" Verb or Helping Verb?

Remember, a helping verb must help another verb. If the verb is not helping another verb, it is the main verb.

Directions: In the sentences below, underline the verb or verb phrase. Write "Helping" if there is a helping verb in the sentence. Write "To Be" if it is the main verb.

___Helping___ 1. She <u>is asking</u> the teacher a question.

___To Be___ 2. Tom <u>was</u> happy to be home.

_____ 3. Mom is making a cake for our party.

_____ 4. I am tired of cartoons.

_____ 5. Dad was singing in the shower.

_____ 6. They were the leaders of our student council.

_____ 7. We are making pictures for the art contest.

_____ 8. He was the strongest person on our team.

Extension: Write three (3) sentences using the words below as "**to be**" verbs. Write three (3) sentences using the words below as **helping** verbs.

is   **are**   **was**

Verbs
#8

I. In the sentences below, underline the verb or verb phrase. Write "Helping" if there is a helping verb in the sentence. Write "To Be" if the to-be verb is the main verb. Write "Action" if it is an action verb.

__**Action**___ 1. Mom <u>made</u> a cake for my birthday.

_____ 2. Jill is sad about Jack's broken crown.

_____ 3. The children were complaining about the food.

_____ 4. We drove all the way to Florida.

_____ 5. I am making a dress for my sister.

_____ 6. The boys wrestled in the back yard for an hour.

_____ 7. Mr. Starr is the driver of the bus.

_____ 8. Mom is shopping with my aunt.

_____ 9. They were ready for the game.

_____ 10. Amy wrote a nice, friendly letter to her cousin.

_____ 11. She is looking for her sweater.

_____ 12. The baby will drink his milk after his nap.

II. Write a story about a party using the helping verbs, "to be" verbs, and action verbs listed below.

Helping verbs: should be waiting   will bring
"To Be" verbs: is   am
Action verbs: opened   wrapped

_____

_____

_____

_____

_____

_____

_____

_____

_____

Adjectives
#1

Adjectives are words that describe nouns.

    Examples: <u>Big</u> basket   <u>Several</u> buildings   <u>Three</u> clowns

Adjectives answer three questions:
    1. **What kind?**   <u>What kind</u> of basket?   <u>Big</u> Basket
    2. **How Much?**   How much money?   <u>Several</u> dollars
    3. **How Many?**   How many clowns?   <u>Three</u> clowns

---

I. Below is a list of adjectives. Write "What kind?", "How Much", or "How Many" next to each adjective.

    1. big - _____

    2. several - _____

    3. four - _____

    4. many - _____

    5. hungry - _____

    6. pretty - _____

    7. small - _____

    8. skinny - _____

    9. tall - _____

    10. some - _____

II. Write three adjectives to describe each noun below.

    1. elephant - _____ _____ _____

    2. pillow - _____ _____ _____

    3. ocean - _____ _____ _____

    4. dog - _____ _____ _____

    5. your neighbor's hair - _____ _____ _____

    6. your best friend - _____ _____ _____

    7. your shirt - _____ _____ _____

    8. your bedroom - _____ _____ _____

    9. snake - _____ _____ _____

    10. circus - _____ _____ _____

Adjectives
#2

I. Below is a list of adjectives. Write "What kind?" "How Much," or "How Many" next to each adjective.

1. large - _____
2. few - _____
3. seven - _____
4. many - _____
5. slimy - _____

6. weird - _____
7. wet - _____
8. hairy - _____
9. short - _____
10. a lot - _____

II. Write three adjectives to describe each noun below.

1. puppy - _____ _____ _____

2. pizza - _____ _____ _____

3. mountains - _____ _____ _____

4. your favorite story - _____ _____ _____

5. a family member - _____ _____ _____

6. your classroom - _____ _____ _____

7. your shoes - _____ _____ _____

8. a concert - _____ _____ _____

9. trash can - _____ _____ _____

10. cotton candy - _____ _____ _____

Extension: Select any five (5) nouns from Part II and write them in sentences. Be sure to use at least one of the adjectives to describe them.

Example: The soft, cuddly puppy played on the floor.

Adjectives
#3

I. Directions: Write an adjective on each line below that fits the sentence.

1. We spent an hour trying to clean the _____ carpet.

2. The girl's _____, _____ hair blew in the wind.

3. I got a _____ present for my birthday. It was a _____ bike.

4. My _____ little sister drove me crazy with her _____ noises.

5. I think that this _____ milk is rotten.

6. We cuddled under our _____, _____ blanket.

7. The _____ clowns sprayed water in the ring master's face.

8. Mom said, "Clean this _____ room right now!"

9. My sister wears the same _____ dress every Friday.

10. The tree was covered with _____, _____ lights.

11. A _____, _____ toad hopped across our yard.

12. At the beach we made _____ sand castles.

II. Write at least five (5) sentences about being in a garden. Describe what you see. Be sure to put at least one adjective in each sentence.

_____

_____

_____

_____

_____

_____

_____

_____

_____

Adjectives
#4

I. Directions: Write an adjective on each line below that fits the sentence.

1. The circus had a _____ elephant and a bunch of _____ monkeys.

2. Our class was so _____ when the principal walked in.

3. For picture day we all wore _____, _____ clothes.

4. A _____ spider made a _____ web in our yard.

5. Andy is a _____ player, but he is too _____ .

6. I just love my _____, _____ pillow.

7. The _____ house felt good after being in the _____ rain.

8. We read a _____ story about a _____ pirate.

9. The climbers kept falling on the _____ ice.

10. The _____ seals made _____ noises so we'd throw them some fish.

11. There was a _____, _____ bear eating our food.

12. Dad warned, "Watch out for _____ animals on your hike."

II. Think of an adjective for each noun below. Write the adjective and noun in a sentence.

1. beach - _____

_____

2. teddy bear - _____

_____

3. watermelon - _____

_____

4. whistle - _____

_____

Adjectives
#5

Comparatives and Superlatives

Adjectives that compare **two things** are called **comparatives**.
Adjectives that compare **three or more things** are called **superlatives**.

Comparatives can be made in two ways:
1. Add "er" to the one syllable adjectives.   big**ger**,   stron**ger**,   fast**er**
2. Add "more" to some two syllable adjectives and all three or more syllable words.   **more** helpful, **more** famous

Superlatives can also be made in two similar ways:
1. Add "est" to the one syllable adjectives.   big**gest**,   stron**gest**,   fast**est**
2. Add "more" to some two syllable adjectives and all three or more syllable words.   **most** helpful, **most** famous

---

I. Fill in the blank with the correct form of each word. *Words break the general rules.

Adjective	Comparative	Superlative
1. intelligent	__more intelligent__	__most intelligent__
2. big	_____	_____
3. calm	_____	_____
4. powerful	_____	_____
5. *messy	_____	_____
6. dark	_____	_____
7. exciting	_____	_____
8. *risky	_____	_____
9. curious	_____	_____
10. *angry	_____	_____
11. small	_____	_____
12. dangerous	_____	_____

Adjectives #6

I. Fill in the blanks with the correct form of each word.

Adjective	Comparative	Superlative
1. good	_____better_____	_____best_____
2. new	_____	_____
3. intelligent	_____	_____
4. patient	_____	_____
5. *grouchy	_____	_____
6. cheap	_____	_____
7. patriotic	_____	_____
8. *dumpy	_____	_____

* What do you notice about all the adjectives that end in Y ?

_____

II. Circle the correct word in each pair. On the line, tell if it is comparative or superlative.

Comparative or Superlative?

__**Superlative**__ 1. This is the (darker , (darkest)) cave of all.

_____ 2. I think turkey is (more tasty , tastier) than ham.

_____ 3. This is the (cleaner , cleanest) shirt in my closet.

_____ 4. Tommy is a (gooder , better) reader than I.

_____ 5. This is the (most funny , funniest) movie I've ever seen.

_____ 6. A snake is (more dangerous , most dangerous) than a spider.

_____ 7. Julie being absent is (more surprising , most surprising) than Kim being late.

_____ 8. Juan is the (nicer , nicest) person in the world.

Extension: Write three (3) sentences about your school using comparatives and three (3) sentences using superlatives. You may use any comparatives and superlatives on this page or make up your own.

Adjectives
#7

I. Directions: Write an adjective on each line below that fits the sentence.

1. The _____ man waited for me to count my money.

2. A _____, _____ balloon floated over our heads.

3. We caught a _____ fish on our camping trip.

4. While hiking we saw a _____ skunk in the bushes.

5. The show was so _____ we laughed for hours.

6. The ball hit the window and sent _____, _____ pieces of glass onto the floor.

7. The bread was too _____ for anyone to eat.

II. Fill in the blanks with the proper comparative or superlative.

(strong)   1. Superman is the _____ person in the world.

(old)   2. My brother is _____ than me.

(messy)   3. Her room is _____ than his room.

(exciting)   4. This is the _____ story I've ever read.

(cheap)   5. A used car is _____ than a new car.

(dangerous) 6. The crocodile is the _____ animal in the river.

(cool)   7. It will be _____ if you sit in the shade.

(intelligent) 8. Patricia is the _____ person at our school.

Extension: Write a story about a fun day at a carnival. Use the adjectives below in your story.

sweet   fast   sour   crunchy   loud

Contractions
#1

Definition: "Contract" means "to shorten." Therefore, a contraction is when two words are shortened into one word. An apostrophe is used to show where letters from one of the words were left out.

Examples: he + is = he's   John + is = John's   you + are = you're

missing i   missing i   missing a

I. The words below are often used to form contractions. Turn the contractions back into the two words.

not   are   will   have   is   am   had   would

1. he'd - _____**he would**_____   6. aren't - _____

2. they're - _____   7. don't - _____

3. I'm - _____   8. it'll - _____

4. you'll - _____   9. should've - _____

5. we're - _____   10. hasn't - _____

II. Turn the words below into contractions.

1. he will - _____**he'll**_____   6. could not - _____

2. they have - _____   7. I have - _____

3. have not - _____   8. she is - _____

4. we will - _____   9. *will not - _____

5. it is - _____   10. cannot - _____

Contractions
#2

Directions: Use the words in the box below to make as many contractions as possible for each word listed.

```
┌─────────────────────────────────┐
│   not    would    am            │
│   are    had           is       │
│        will    have             │
└─────────────────────────────────┘
```

Example:

She - __she'd__(she would)   __she'd__(she had)   __she'll__   __she's__

1. he - _____ _____ _____ _____

2. they - _____ _____ _____ _____ _____

3. I - _____ _____ _____ _____

4. you - _____ _____ _____ _____ _____

5. we - _____ _____ _____ _____ _____

6. could - _____ _____   11. will - _____

7. it - _____ _____   12. are - _____

8. should - _____ _____   13. has - _____

9. would - _____ _____   14. did - _____

10. do - _____   15. have - _____

Extension: Write five (5) sentences using the contractions below.

it's   don't   you're   we'll   I'm

Contractions
#3

> ### Two Tricky Contractions
>
> What words make up **can't** and **won't**?
>
> Can't should be "can not" and won't should be "wo not". Here's how they really look: **can't = cannot**   **won't = will not**

I. Write "cannot" or "will not" on the lines below. Next, write "can't" or "won't" below the line.

1. She ___**cannot**___ help me with my homework.
   can't

2. The cake _____ be ready until 8:00.

3. Our kitten _____ get out of the tree.

4. The boss _____ take "no" for an answer.

5. I _____ study with the television on.

6. The children _____ play with you if you are not nice.

7. Johnny is sick so he _____ go to school.

8. No matter how hard I scrub, the stain _____ come out.

9. The baby _____ sleep because he's sick.

10. Cindy _____ come out of the bathroom.

II. Change the contractions below into two words.

1. Amy's - _____**Amy is**_____   6. won't - _____

2. John'll - _____   7. hasn't - _____

3. can't - _____   8. I'm - _____

4. they're - _____   9. would've - _____

5. you've - _____   10. we're - _____

Contractions
#4

Contraction Danger

Be careful never to use negative words like **no, never**, and **nothing** with a contraction that ends in **n't**.

Incorrect	**Correct**
She would**n't** like **no** ice cream.	She would**n't** like **any** ice cream.
He **doesn't never** lie.	He **doesn't ever** lie.
They **aren't** doing **nothing** tonight.	They **aren't** doing **anything** tonight.

I. Rewrite each sentence correctly.

1. We don't need to bring nothing to the party.

    _____

2. Hazel won't let nobody ride her bike.

    _____

3. He can't never make that work.

    _____

4. The police wouldn't let no cars go into the lot.

    _____

5. This game doesn't never work properly.

    _____

6. My sister isn't never ready on time.

    _____

7. He didn't want no olives on his pizza.

    _____

8. Dad won't let no one use his camera again.

    _____

Extension: Write five (5) sentences using the contractions below.

can't   won't   isn't   didn't   weren't

Contractions
#5

I. Write contractions that fit the sentences on the lines below. Use the contractions in the box or make up your own.

she's	don't	you'll	can't	won't	I'm	aren't	it'll
hasn't	wouldn't	they'll	we've	he'll	didn't	we'll	

1. Everyone said that ___**she's**___ the best singer.

2. They _____ ready to go yet.

3. Mom asked, "_____ it be nice if we all took a picture together?"

4. _____ need to get up early tomorrow.

5. _____ make any noise or _____ wake the baby.

6. Whenever _____ hungry I make a sandwich.

7. She _____ see so she is changing seats.

8. _____ be a long time before _____ argue with me again.

9. He told the teacher that he _____ make the mess.

10. Tina _____ help us clean the house.

11. We were ready to go, but Tim _____ put his shoes on.

12. _____ written many cards, and _____ deliver them tomorrow.

II. Turn the words below into contractions.

1. he will - _____**he'll**_____   6. I will - _____

2. they have - _____   7. they are - _____

3. will not - _____   8. cannot - _____

4. they would - _____   9. you are - _____

5. were not - _____   10. do not - _____

Contractions
#6

I. Write contractions that fit the sentences on the lines below. Use the contractions in the box or make up your own.

haven't   don't   shouldn't   can't   you'll   aren't   it's
we'll   I'll   isn't   wouldn't   you're   won't   hasn't

1. We promise that we _____ make fun of your new hair cut.

2. They _____ putting any candles on the birthday cake.

3. _____ make the beds if _____ clean the toilets.

4. She said that she _____ going to play.

5. Dad _____ clean the yard until he buys a new rake.

6. Kelly _____ let anyone touch her new necklace.

7. _____ we be in class right now?

8. _____ going to lose your place in line if you _____ come back.

9. If he _____ fixed the car by tomorrow, _____ walk to school.

10. _____ not a good idea to swim if you _____ taken lessons.

II. Rewrite the contractions below.

1. he'll - _____**he will**_____
2. they'd - _____
3. hasn't - _____
4. can't - _____
5. don't - _____

6. there's - _____
7. won't - _____
8. could've - _____
9. I'm - _____
10. weren't - _____

Extension: You lost your favorite toy. Write a story about how you found it. Use any five (5) contractions in your story.

Chapter 3
Review

I. Pronouns

Write the definition of a pronoun:

_____

Directions: Rewrite the sentences by changing the underlined nouns to pronouns.

1. <u>Lupe</u> gave a <u>present</u> to <u>Gena</u>.

    ____**She** gave **it** to **her**._____

2. <u>Dad</u> made <u>paper airplanes</u> for <u>Sammy and me</u>.

    _____

3. <u>The teachers</u> let the <u>students</u> have a <u>snack</u>.

    _____

4. <u>Amy</u> gave <u>Ben's</u> book to <u>John</u>.

    _____

5. <u>Marco and I</u> played checkers with our <u>friends</u>.

    _____

6. <u>Nancy and Carrie</u> borrowed <u>Cindy's</u> chairs for the <u>party</u>.

    _____

II. Verbs: Past, Present, and Future

Directions: Write the past, present, and future tense for the words below.

	Past Tense	Present Tense	Future Tense
1. sing -	_____	_____	_____
2. thought -	_____	_____	_____
3. read -	_____	_____	_____
4. will type -	_____	_____	_____
5. fight -	_____	_____	_____

III. Adjectives

A. Directions: Write three adjectives to describe each noun below.

1. puppy - _____ _____ _____

2. pizza - _____ _____ _____

3. mountains - _____ _____ _____

B. Directions: Change each adjective into a comparative and superlative.

Adjective	Comparative	Superlative
1. good	_____better_____	_____best_____
2. new	_____	_____
3. intelligent	_____	_____

IV. Contractions

A. Directions: Write the words below as a contraction.

1. cannot - _____   4. you are - _____

2. will not - _____   5. is not - _____

3. you have - _____   6. it is - _____

B. Fix each sentence below:

1. The camera didn't have no film in it.

_____

2. We won't never get there.

_____

Unit 4

Comma Rules

Dates

City, State

Lists

Adjectives

Letters

_____

Student

Comma Rules

	Mastery	Non-Mastery
1. Dates		
2. City, State / Addresses		
3. Lists		
4. Adjectives		
5. Letters		

Name: _____

Comma Rules
Dates
#1

What day were you born? If you say, "I was born on the 11th," you have left out an important piece of information - the month! Therefore, when you tell what day something happens, you need to include the month.

Rule #1: Day, Year -   January 1, 2008   June 30, 1775

* Do not put a comma
   after the month if no   January 2008   June 1775
   day is used.

— · — · · — · · — · — · — · — · — · · — · — · · — · — · — · · — · · — · · — · · —

Directions: Place commas where they are needed. Next, rewrite the day and year on the line below. * Watch out for months without a day.

A. March 3 2008   B. October 2007   C. December 25 2000

  March 3, 2008   **_October 2007_**   _____

D. January 1 2010   E. April 8 1841   F. May 2005

_____   _____   _____

G. November 25 2002   H. February 2012   I. October 31 2007

_____   _____   _____

J. August 2004   K. December 31 1999   L. March 5 2005

_____   _____   _____

M. June 28 1824   N. May 18 2006   O. July 2015

_____   _____   _____

Comma Rules
Dates
#2

I. Place commas where they are needed. Next, rewrite the day and year on the line below. * Watch out for months without a day.

A. March 3 2008	B. October 2007	C. December 25 2000
**March 3, 2008**	_**October 2007**_	_____

D. June 27 2004	E. September 1 1986	F. February 1922
_____	_____	_____

G. August 2009	H. January 4 2005	I. March 9 2007
_____	_____	_____

J. April 30 1845	K. May 1776	L. July 4 1776
_____	_____	_____

II. Place commas in the story below where they are needed.

I was born on December 15 2000. My brother was born on January 16 2001, and my sister was born on February 17 2002. Can you guess when my dad was born? He was born on March 18 1973. My mom? She was born in April 1974, but she was born on the 6th. We all say that she spoiled the pattern. It would have been neat if she was born on the 14th or the 19th. At least the month fits the pattern. The funny thing is that our dog was born in May 2004 and our cat was born in June 2005. Another interesting fact is that my aunt had her baby on July 19 2005, and my uncle was born on August 20 1974. Does this mean anything? Maybe not, but it sure is weird.

> **Extension:** Write each date below in a sentence. Be sure only to put commas where they are needed.
>
> May 1 2007 / December 25 2010 / September 2008 / June 23 2009

Comma Rules
City, State / Addresses
#1

Rule #2: City, State – Place a **comma (,)** between the city and state.

Examples: Phoenix, Arizona   Lakewood, California

Rule #3: Address – Use a **comma** after the street address, the city, and the state.

Example: 555 Flower Street, Bellflower, California
                   street address   city   state

— — – – — — – – — — – – — — – – — — – – — — – – — — – – — — – – — — – – — — – – —

I. Place commas where they are needed. Next, rewrite the city, state or address on the line below.

A. Los Angeles California

Los Angeles, California

B. 321 Main Street Orange Florida

321 Main Street, Orange, Florida

C. 11408 E. 211ᵗʰ Tulane OH

_____

D. Miami Florida

_____

E. Sacramento California

_____

F. 241 Jersey Way Denver Colorado

_____

G. 949 Arbor St. Franklin TN

_____

H. Houston Texas

_____

I. Portland Oregon

_____

J. 3305 Lees Ave. Atlanta Georgia

_____

K. 13 Big St. Kona Hawaii

_____

L. Las Vegas Nevada

_____

Comma Rules
City, State / Addresses
#2

I. Place commas where they are needed. Next, rewrite the city, state or address on the line below.

A. Boise Idaho

_____***Boise, Idaho***_____

B. 14732 Bowling Lane   Chicago Illinois

*14732 Bowling Lane, Chicago, Illinois*

C. 484 East St. Augusta Maine

_____

D. Minneapolis Minnesota

_____

E. Lincoln Nebraska

_____

F. 15243 West Point Albany New York

_____

G. 9185 Main Ave. Toledo OH

_____

H. Hershey Pennsylvania

_____

I. Salt Lake City Utah

_____

J. 22448 Kite St. Helena Montana

_____

II. Place commas in the story below where they are needed.

This summer my family is going to Springfield Missouri to visit my cousins. They just bought a new house. Their address is 327 Viking Way Galloway Missouri. It's just south of Springfield. On our way we hope to visit Flagstaff Arizona and see the Grand Canyon. We would also like to stop in San Antonio Texas to see the Alamo. While I'm gone I'm sending postcards to my friend Amy who lives at 323 Heart St. Bellflower California. I'll also send one to my grandma who lives on 4545 Henrilee Ave. Lawton Oklahoma.

Extension: How many cities and states can you name? Use a map to help you find five (5) cities from five (5) different states. List all five cities and their states. Be sure to put a comma between the city and state.

Example: Miami, Florida

Comma Rules
Dates / City, State / Addresses
Mixed Review

I. Place commas where they are needed. * Watch out for months without a day.

1. On April 22 2004 we went to Honolulu Hawaii.

2. Vacation started early in June 2003.

3. The contest said the letter arrived on April 5 2003 at 4531 E. Arlington Rd. Dallas Texas.

4. On May 3 1920 a plane made it from San Diego CA to Long Island New York.

5. Our family moved to 222 Washington Rd. Seal Beach CA in November 1988.

6. Santa lives at 123 Gum Drop Lane North Pole Alaska, I think.

7. In June 2006 the Olympic committee announced that the Olympics would be in Atlanta Georgia, and they will begin on February 2 2010.

8. The best time to visit our cabin at 396 Big Bear Ave. Arrowhead CA would be in July 2006

II. Write each item below in a sentence. Put commas where they are needed.

1. October 31 2010 - _____

   _____

2. Brooklyn New York - _____

   _____

3. 1314 Love Ave. Lakewood Colorado - _____

   _____

4. June 2012 - _____

   _____

5. August 12 2008 - _____

   _____

6. 555 Hope Ave. Little Rock Arkansas - _____

   _____

85

Comma Rules
Lists
#1

Rule #4: Lists

Use **commas (,)** to separate three or more items in a list. Do not put a comma after the last item in the list.

Examples:

Mom bought me some <u>pencils, crayons, paper, and glue</u> for school.

Alyssa gave a Valentine's Day card to <u>Shawn, Ryan, and Tim</u>.

_____

Directions: Put **commas (,)** after items in a list. Use a crayon to highlight the list.

1. We learned about the moon stars and planets in science.

2. There are scissors crayons and pencils on your table.

3. It seems like we read write and study all day.

4. Amy Sally and Melissa are best friends.

5. Mom told me to wash rinse and dry the dishes.

6. The store was out of chocolate vanilla and strawberry ice cream.

7. Our new puppy has chewed up my slippers socks dolls and homework.

8. We put milk butter sugar and flour into the recipe.

9. David Joy Shawna and Ryan are on the same team.

10. My mom's favorite holidays are Christmas Easter 4th of July and Thanksgiving.

11. We need to put spoons knives and forks on the table.

12. Leaves twigs and trash blew onto our yard.

13. Johnny has a fish dog mouse and lizard for a pet.

14. The show will start when the teachers students and parents enter.

15. Our team needs a new pitcher catcher and captain.

Comma Rules
Lists
#2

I. Place commas where they are needed. Use a crayon to highlight the list.

1. The story was about how a bird mouse and snake became friends.

2. The sun causes wind rain hurricanes and tornadoes.

3. Police fire-fighters and paramedics participated in the assembly.

4. We need glue scissors and tissue for our art project.

5. Washington Adams and Jefferson were our first presidents.

6. My dad is afraid of snakes spiders and mice.

7. Today I wrote revised and edited my report.

8. Her baby brother likes to be tickled on his belly feet and chin.

9. Mr. Alexander taught us about health science and history.

10. Along the beach were sand castles children and seaweed.

II. Write the items below in a sentence. Be sure to use them as a list, and place commas where they are needed.

1. (pizza / popcorn / soda)

   _____

2. (movies / video games / sports)

   _____

3. (Molly / Mary / Linda)

   _____

4. (rabbit / squirrel / skunk)

   _____

5. (walk / jog / sprint / run)

   _____

Comma Rules
Lists
#3

Directions: Write the items below in a sentence. Be sure to use them as a list, and place commas where they are needed. You may use "and" or "or" to connect the words.

1. (computer / television / VCR)

    _____

2. (field trip / assembly / party)

    _____

3. (pencil / paper / eraser)

    _____

4. (friends / neighbors / relatives)

    _____

5. (cake / ice cream / popcorn)

    _____

6. (potatoes / corn / turkey)

    _____

7. (soccer / tennis / football)

    _____

8. (flower / tree / plant)

    _____

Extension: Write five sentences about things you use in each room of your house. Be sure to use items in a list in each sentence.

Comma Rules
Adjectives
#1

Rule #5: Adjectives

When you put more than one adjective in front of a noun, you need to put

commas (,) to separate the list of adjectives.

Examples:

1. There was a <u>soft, cute, furry puppy</u> in the window of the store.

2. I love to eat <u>smooth, creamy peanut</u> butter.

Look at Example #2. What is the difference between putting a comma in "Items in a List" and "Adjectives"?

Answer: There needs to be three (3) items in a list before you can use commas. However, you need to place a comma even if there are only two adjectives before a noun. Also, there is no "and."

— · · — — · · — — · — · · — — · · — — · — · · — — · · — — · — · · — — · · — — · · ·

Directions: Put **commas (,)** between the adjectives. Use a crayon to highlight the adjectives and the words they describe.

1. There were many bright colorful lights around the tree.

2. The strong brave workers saved the girl from the burning building.

3. We walked into the room and saw short busy elves making toys.

4. All the girls were wearing long clean colorful dresses.

5. The whining complaining children were ready for a nap.

6. We used our tongues to lick the sweet sticky syrup from our mouths.

7. The clown's thick curly colorful hair made him look funny.

8. Amy has small fuzzy animals all over her bed.

9. Many hungry dirty lumberjacks came into the restaurant.

10. Captain Hook was a mean nasty cheating no-good worthless pirate.

Comma Rules
Adjectives
#2

I. Put **commas (,)** between the adjectives. Use a crayon to highlight the adjectives and the words they describe.

1. We worked for two long hard hours on this puzzle.

2. Our new neighbors have two nice cheerful children.

3. Mom said it was time to throw away these old dirty shirts.

4. The dark flat clouds made their way across the sky.

5. Her tiny broken umbrella couldn't keep the cold sharp rain away.

6. The young handsome soldiers marched in the parade.

7. The song had a fun bouncy sound to it.

8. Yvette has such long dark beautiful hair.

9. The long boring game seemed to last forever.

10. The wild crazy boys destroyed the room.

Directions: Write the adjectives and nouns below in a sentence. Be sure to place commas where they are needed.

1. (cold hard floor)

_____

2. (big heavy shelf)

_____

3. (quick slippery lizard)

_____

4. (soft smooth blanket)

_____

5. (long wooden fence)

_____

Comma Rules
Adjectives
#3

Directions: Write the adjectives and nouns below in a sentence. Be sure to place commas where they are needed.

1. (soft comfortable chair)

   _____

2. (rich famous movie star)

   _____

3. (plump jolly baby)

   _____

4. (delicious healthy snack)

   _____

5. (fun silly clown)

   _____

6. (cool refreshing water)

   _____

7. (big round bubble)

   _____

8. (long thin tail)

   _____

Extension: Use the list of adjectives below to write five (5) sentences about a circus. Use two or three adjectives to describe something in each sentence. Put the adjectives in front of the word they describe. Be sure to put commas where they are needed.

<u>Adjectives</u>

funny   big   floppy   bouncy   fast   crunchy   delicious

colorful   exciting   thrilling   dangerous   happy   smiling

short   fat   crazy   graceful   brave   skillful

* Use any other adjectives that come to mind.

Comma Rules
Friendly Letter
#1

Rule #6: Greeting

Place a **comma (,)** after the greeting in a friendly letter.
Examples:

    Dear Maria,   Dear Jose,   Dear Arthur,

Rule #7: Closing

Place a **comma (,)** after the closing in a friendly letter.
Examples:

    Yours truly,   Sincerely,   Friends forever,

Directions: Put **commas (,)** after the greeting and closing in the letters below. Write the word "Greeting" next to the greeting and "Closing" next to the closing.

1. Dear Nemo,
        Stay there. Your dad is on his way.   **Greeting**
            Sincerely,   **Closing**
            Dori

2. Dear Shrek
        See you at the swamp. I'll make the waffles.
            Your friend   _____
            Donkey

3. Dear Belle
        Did you like the book Where the Wild Things Are?
            Truly yours   _____
            Beast

4. Dear Woody
        Remember when you pushed me out of the window?
            Best wishes   _____
            Buzz

5. Dear Sulley
        Don't forget to return Boo to her house today.
            Your friend   _____
            Mike

Comma Rules
Friendly Letter
#2

I. Put **commas (,)** after the greeting and closing in the letters below. Write the word "Greeting" next to the greeting and "Closing" next to the closing.

1. Dear Mrs. Clause   _____
      Please send Rudolf. There's heavy fog tonight.
                    Sincerely   _____
                    Dasher

2. Dear Captain Hook   _____
      Sorry about the hand. Say hi to Crock for me.
                    Your friend   _____
                    Peter

3. Dear Pumbaa   _____
      How about cutting down on the beans?
                    Your buddy   _____
                    Timon

II. Write one-sentence letters to your friends. Use the lines below to help you place the greeting, body, closing, and signature in the correct place. Don't forget to place commas where they are needed.

1. _____

      _____

                                   _____

                                   _____

2. _____

      _____

                                   _____

                                   _____

Comma Rules
Friendly Letter
#3

Directions: Write one-sentence letters to your friends. Tell your friend something that you like about him or her. Use the lines below to help you place the greeting, body, closing, and signature in the correct place. Don't forget to place commas where they are needed.

1. _____

   _____

   _____

   _____

2. _____

   _____

   _____

3. _____

   _____

   _____

4. _____

   _____

   _____

   _____

Extension: Pretend that you are any cartoon character. Write three (3) friendly letters to any other cartoon characters. Each letter only needs to be one or two sentences. Be sure to put commas where they are needed.

Comma Rules
Mixed Review
#1

Rule #1: Day, Year   **Rule #4: Lists**   **Rule #6: Greeting**

Rule #2: City, State   **Rule #5: Adjectives**   **Rule #7: Closing**

Rule #3: Address

I. Place commas where they are needed. Write the name of the rule below each comma.

1. There was a wild**,** exciting party on January 1**,** 2004.
    Adjectives   **Day, Year**
2. San Francisco California is famous for earthquakes hills houses and bridges.

3. Dear Porky

        In April 2012 meet me outside your house with a bottle of ketchup.

                                                            Your friend

                                                            B.B. Wolf

4. A soft cuddly bunny will enjoy a carrot radish or lettuce.

5. Williamsburg Virginia was a big crowded city on July 4 1776.

6. Dear Mickey

        You have the cutest large round ears.

                                                            Sincerely

                                                            Minnie

7. On May 19 1968 the moon earth and sun lined up.

8. A large hairy spider was found at 222 W. Palm Dr. in Miami Florida.

Extension: Write a sentence about each family member. Tell where they were born (city, state) and when they were born (day, year).

   Example: My dad was born in Spokane, Washington on August 15, 1971.

* Note: If your parents were born in a different country, write about the day they arrived in the United States.

Comma Rules
Mixed Review
#2

Rule #1: Day, Year   **Rule #4: Lists**   **Rule #6: Greeting**

Rule #2: City, State   **Rule #5: Adjectives**   **Rule #7: Closing**

Rule #3: Address

I. Place commas where they are needed. Write the name of the rule below each comma.

1. My dad proposed to my mom in Lincoln Nebraska on February 14 2000.

2. Dear Martha

   The soldiers just loved the biscuits gravy and jam.

   Love

   George W.

3. There was a concert in Denver Colorado in December 2001.

4. Mail the coupon to 293 Broadway Mobile Alabama for a free prize picture and autograph.

5. The fastest strongest wolf usually becomes the leader of the pack.

6. Dear Thomas

   My new address is 484 Eastern St. Brain Tree Massachusetts.

   Sincerely

   John

7. The silly entertaining clown wore a funny hat shoes and pants.

8. Parents can send post cards presents and treats to their children at 11934 Pine Ave. Crestline California.

Extension: Find the address of five friends or relatives. Write them each in a sentence. Be sure to use commas correctly.

Comma Rules
Mixed Review
#3

Rule #1: Day, Year   **Rule #4: Lists**   **Rule #6: Greeting**

Rule #2: City, State   **Rule #5: Adjectives**   **Rule #7: Closing**

Rule #3: Address

I. Place commas where they are needed. Write the name of the rule below each comma.

1. The address on the birthday invitation said 427 Stevely Branson Iowa.

2. She had cookies cake and ice cream at her party.

3. Old cartoons ended in December 2004, but started again on January 3 2004.

4. This summer we're going to St. Louis Missouri.

5. Mom put a large fluffy pancake on my plate.

6. Dear Rabbit

   You have such a beautiful peaceful garden.

   Yours truly

   Pooh

7. We love to run jump and slide in the snow.

8. My first house was 724 Ram St. Tulsa Oklahoma.

9. Is the happiest place on earth Anaheim California or Orlando Florida.

10. The Super Bowl was on February 6 2005.

Extension:

1. Think about three (3) people you know. Write a birthday wish list for each person. Use commas in your lists.

   Example: Amy wants a doll, clothes, and a puppy.

2. Write three (3) sentences about things you want for your birthday. Use two adjectives before each noun.

   Example: I want a cute, cuddly puppy.

Comma Rules
Mixed Review
#4

Rule #1: Day, Year   **Rule #4: Lists**   **Rule #6: Greeting**

Rule #2: City, State   **Rule #5: Adjectives**   **Rule #7: Closing**

Rule #3: Address

I. Place commas where they are needed. Write the name of the rule below each comma.

1. The beautiful ancient tradition of Chanukah began on December 8 2004.

2. The furniture clothes and dishes will be delivered to 374 Main St Richmond Virginia.

3. Dear Ariel

   Do you give singing lessons? You have such an amazing angelic voice.

   Sincerely yours

   E. Fudd

4. There were floats bands and horses at the New Year's Day Parade on January 1 2003.

5. Brilliant hard-working scientists predict that there will be a colony on Mars by December 2050.

6. Dear Mr. Troll

   Sorry about that whole bridge thing. I hope your head feels better.

   Yours truly

   Bill Goat

Extension: Think of any three (3) characters from any stories that you have read. Write three (3) letters, one or two sentences long, that these characters might write to someone else in their story.

For example, in <u>Charlotte's Web</u>, Wilbur might write a letter to Charlotte, thanking her for her help.

Be sure to use commas in your greeting and closing.

Unit 5

Four Types of Sentences

Subjects and Predicates

Finding Subjects and Predicates

Student

	Mastery	Non-Mastery
1. Four Types of Sentences		
2. Subjects and Predicates		
3. Finding Subjects and Predicates		

Four Types of Sentences
#1

Name: _____

1. **Declarative Sentence**: This type of sentence states a fact. It ends with a period. (.)

Examples:

The movie starts at eight o'clo<u>ck.</u>

Once upon a time there were three bea<u>rs.</u>

The Trick: Think of a Southern belle. A Southern belle is a very proper young woman. Draw a picture of her saying, " I declare! I am making a declarative sentence."

Declarative Sentence

---

2. **Interrogative Sentence:** This type of sentence asks a question. It ends with a question mark. (**?**)

Examples:

Where are you going **?**
Who is the best player on the team**?**

The Trick: When the police ask a suspected criminal some questions, they are "interrogating" him. Draw a picture of a police officer interrogating, or questioning, a prisoner under two hot lights.

Interrogative Sentence

Directions: If the sentence is declarative, write "Declarative". If the sentence is interrogative, write "Interrogative". Put a period or question mark at the end.

_____ 1. Where are you going____

_____ 2. I'm going to the store____

_____ 3. There's a sale on shirts____

_____ 4. How much are the shirts____

_____ 5. You can get two shirts for fifteen dollars____

Four Types of Sentences
#2

What is a declarative sentence? _____

What is an interrogative sentence? _____

I. If the sentence is declarative, write "Declarative". If the sentence is interrogative, write "Interrogative". Put a period or question mark at the end.

_____ 1. The male emperor penguin sits on the egg____

_____ 2. How long does it take for the egg to hatch____

_____ 3. The egg rests on the penguin's toes for sixty-five days____

_____ 4. The mother leaves to feed in the ocean____

_____ 5. Will the mother penguin return____

_____ 6. Suzie asked, "When will the father penguin eat____"

_____ 7. Many penguins bunch together to stay warm____

_____ 8. Warm penguins on the inside let the outside penguins

   come to the center____

_____ 9. Can the emperor penguin fly____

_____ 10. These penguins can't fly, but they are great swimmers ____

II. Pretend that there was an argument at school. The teacher is trying to figure out what happened. Write interrogative sentences a teacher might ask. Next, write declarative statements a student might say in response.

1. Interrogative: _____

   Declarative: _____

2. Interrogative: _____

   Declarative: _____

3. Interrogative: _____

   Declarative: _____

4. Interrogative: _____

   Declarative: _____

Four Types of Sentences
#3

Exclamatory Sentence

1. **Exclamatory Sentence**: This type of sentence states strong feeling or emotion. It ends with an exclamation point. (!)

Examples:

Hurry! The movie starts in ten minutes !

Watch out for that car !

The Trick: Draw a picture of someone kicking the winning goal at a soccer game. Write: "We're champions !" exclaimed Jose.

2. **Imperative Sentence:** This type of sentence gives a command or makes a request. It ends with a period. (.)

Examples:

Wait for me.
Please put that on the table.

The Trick: Draw two people having a conversation. One person says, "Tell me what an imperative is." The other person says, "You just said an imperative." The first person says, "Tell me what I said." The other responds, " You just did it again."

Imperative Sentence

Directions: If the sentence is exclamatory, write "Exclamatory". If the sentence is imperative, write "Imperative". Put a period or exclamation point at the end.

_____ 1. Watch your step____

_____ 2. The house is on fire____

_____ 3. The British are coming____

_____ 4. Please save a piece for me____

_____ 5. Take out a piece of paper____

Four Types of Sentences
#4

Name: _____

What is an exclamatory sentence? _____

What is an imperative sentence? _____

I. If the sentence is exclamatory, write "Exclamatory." If the sentence is imperative, write "Imperative." Put a period or exclamation point at the end.

_____ 1. The crowd shouted, "We're not going to take it anymore____"

_____ 2. Make your bed before you go to school____

_____ 3. We just won a million dollars____

_____ 4. Stop bothering your brother____

_____ 5. Wait for me outside your school____

_____ 6. I need a doctor in here, now____

_____ 7. "They're going to be late if we don't hurry____" screamed Amy.

_____ 8. Hurry up please____

_____ 9. Finish your homework when you get home from school____

_____ 10. The water is overflowing out of the tub____

II. There's a fire and some fire fighters are working hard. Write three (3) exclamatory sentences that someone might say at the fire. Next, write three (3) imperative sentences the chief fire fighter might say.

Exclamatory Sentences

1. _____

2. _____

3. _____

Imperative Sentences

1. _____

2. _____

3. _____

Four Types of Sentences
#5

What is an interrogative sentence? _____

What is an imperative sentence? _____

I. Write Declarative, Interrogative, Exclamatory, or Imperative next to each
   sentence. Put a period, exclamation point, or question mark at the end.

_____ 1. Don't killer whales hunt together in packs____

_____ 2. Killer whales will eat walruses, seals, and sea turtles____

_____ 3. "I see a killer whale____" shouted the ship's captain.

_____ 4. Listen to the sound the whale makes____

_____ 5. Jenny yelled excitedly, "The whale just caught a fish____"

_____ 6. How do killer whales trap and eat land animals____

_____ 7. Killer whales use their tails to splash animals into the water____

_____ 8. "Killer whales are cool____" shouted Tommy.

_____ 9. Look at the white spot around the whale's eye____

_____ 10. These whales swallow their food whole without chewing____

_____ 11. Aren't killer whales also called orcas____

II. Write four (4) exclamatory sentences that a rescue worker would say after an
    earthquake. End each sentence with "exclaimed the worker."

   Example: "If you're homeless, go to the shelter!" exclaimed the worker.

1. _____

   _____

2. _____

   _____

3. _____

   _____

4. _____

   _____

Four Types of Sentences
#6

What is a declarative sentence? _____

What is an exclamatory sentence? _____

I. Directions: Write Declarative, Interrogative, Exclamatory, or Imperative next to each sentence. Put a period, exclamation point, or question mark at the end.

_____ 1. Listen to these facts about koalas____

_____ 2. Koalas are marsupials and carry their babies in pouches____

_____ 3. "The baby koala is so cute____" exclaimed Nancy.

_____ 4. How old are baby koalas when they leave the pouch____

_____ 5. Look how the koala eats the eucalyptus leaves____

_____ 6. After seven months, the koala is old enough to leave the pouch____

_____ 7. Read more about koalas at your library____

_____ 8. Newborn koalas are the size of a jellybean____

_____ 9. What is a koala's favorite food____

_____ 10. "We need to protect the koalas____" shouted the protesters.

_____ 11. A shocked Paul yelled, "That koala just jumped to another tree___"

_____ 12. Where did you learn so much about koalas____

II. Write four (4) imperative sentences that a teacher might say.

Example: "Put your homework in the basket" requested the teacher.

1. _____

   _____

2. _____

   _____

3. _____

   _____

4. _____

   _____

Subjects and Predicates

For the Teacher:

For many third graders, thinking about subjects and predicates is a new way of looking at sentences. Before doing any of these worksheets, the teacher needs to go over the definitions of subjects (the who or what of the sentence) and predicates (what the subject is or does). Once they understand the definitions, the worksheets will give them examples of subjects and predicates in action. By finding subjects and predicates within simple sentences, the students will be ready to write more complex sentences without the fear of creating run-ons.

Introduce the Idea:

Part I – The Subject

1. Write a short sentence on the board or on sentence strips.
2. Ask the students to find the subject of the sentence.
3. Add adjectives and prepositional phrases to the sentence. Ask the students if the subject has changed.
4. Put phrases in front of the sentence. Ask the students if the subject is the same.
5. Review the definition of a subject:
    a. Have the students say "subject" five times.
    b. Chant: "Who or what the sentence is about."

Example A for the students:

1. The dog barked.

2. Subject = dog

3. The big, ugly dog barked at the mailman.   The subject is still "dog".

4. In the front yard the big, ugly dog barked at the mailman.   The subject is still "dog".

5. "Dog" is always the who or what of the sentence.

Example B for the students:

1. The dress is pretty.

2. Subject = dress

3. The dress in the window is pretty. The subject is still "dress".

4. The pink flowery dress in the window is pretty.   The subject is still "dog".

5. "Dress" is always the what of the sentence.

* Now, do Subject Worksheets #1 - #3

Part II – The Predicate

Repeat steps #1- #5 again. This time focus on the predicate. Now that the students know the subject, they can figure out what the subject is or does.

1. Write a short sentence on the board or on sentence strips.

2. Ask the students to find the predicate of the sentence.

3. Add adjectives and prepositional phrases to the sentence. Ask the students if the predicate has changed.

4. Put phrases in front of the sentence. Ask the students if the predicate is the same.

5. Review the definition of a predicate:

    a. Have the students say "predicate" five times.

    b. Chant: "What the subject is or does."

Example A for the students:

1. The dog barked.

2. Predicate = barked

3. The big, ugly dog barked at the mailman.   The predicate is still "barked".

4. In the front yard the big, ugly dog barked at the mailman.   The predicate is still "barked".

5. "Barked" is always what the subject does.

Example B for the students:

1. The dress is pretty.

2. Predicate = is pretty

3. The dress in the window is pretty.   The predicate is still "is pretty".

4. The pink flowery dress in the window is pretty.   The predicate is still "is pretty".

5. "Is pretty" is always the "is" of the sentence.

* Now, do Predicate Worksheets #1 - #3

Subjects
#1

> **Subject:** The who or what of the sentence.
>
> To find the subject of any sentence, ask yourself, "What is the who or what of the sentence?"
>
> Example: **The bird flew away.**
>
> Who or what is this sentence about?   Bird
>
> **When the cat came around, the bird flew away.**
>
> Is the subject cat or bird? Remember, this sentence is still about the bird. It is about what the bird did when the cat came around. Therefore, the subject is still "bird".

I. Subjects: Who or What?

Directions: Is each subject below a who or a what? Write "who" or "what" next to each word.

_____	1. Mrs. Garcia	_____	6. they
_____	2. ice	_____	7. hammer
_____	3. (it)	_____	8. button
_____	4. student	_____	9. singer
_____	5. trees	_____	10. tractor

II. Find the Subject

Directions: Write the subject of each sentence on the line.

_____ 1. Mrs. Garcia is my teacher.

_____ 2. The pencil belongs to Mrs. Garcia.

_____ 3. The ice is melting in the sun.

_____ 4. A girl needs ice for her drink.

_____ 5. Our tree loses most of its leaves in December.

_____ 6. A bird fell out of the tree.

_____ 7. Dad used a hammer to fix the fence.

_____ 8. The hammer fell on my foot.

_____ 9. A button came off of my shirt.

_____ 10. Mom sewed the button back on my shirt.

Subjects
#2

The subject is the _____ or _____ of the sentence.

I. Subjects: Who or What?
   Directions: Is each subject below a who or a what? Write "who" or "what" next to each word.

   _____ 1. bird   _____ 6. love

   _____ 2. friend   _____ 7. photographer

   _____ 3. pencil   _____ 8. helper

   _____ 4. teacher   _____ 9. paper

   _____ 5. parent   _____ 10. idea

II. Circle the subject in each sentence. If the subject is a "who," write "who" on the line. If the subject is a "what," write "what" on the line.

   1. The radio played music all night.   _____

   2. Music played on the radio all night.   _____

   3. After the concert Mr. Jones smiled.   _____

   4. The concert was enjoyed by Mr. Jones.   _____

   5. A big, mean, angry wrestler threw a chair into the crowd.

   _____

   6. The crowd threw the chair back at the wrestler.   _____

   7. Love can solve so many problems.   _____

   8. The room was filled with a lot of love.   _____

   9. The paper fell onto the floor.   _____

   10. You need to write your name on the paper.   _____

Name: _____

Subjects
#3

What is a subject? _____

I. Subjects: Who or What?
   Directions: Is each subject below a who or a what? Write "who" or "what"
   next to each word.

_____ 1. he		_____ 6. dollar
_____ 2. fork		_____ 7. leader
_____ 3. doll		_____ 8. memory
_____ 4. it		_____ 9. music
_____ 5. sailor		_____ 10. farmer

II. Circle the subject in each sentence. If the subject is a "who," write "who"
   on the line. If the subject is a "what," write "what" on the line.

1. He told him about the party. _____

2. A party would be a lot of fun. _____

3. The fork fell onto the floor. _____

4. It needed to be cleaned. _____

5. A cute, little doll rested on the bed. _____

6. The bed had a cute little doll on it. _____

7. Only a dollar is needed to ride on the train. _____

8. The ride only costs a dollar. _____

9. Her memory is very good. _____

10. Jay has a very good memory. _____

Extension: Write five (5) sentences using the words below as subjects.
Underline the word in your sentence.

   Example: The <u>water</u> spilled on the floor.

   water   coach   book   friend   game

111

Predicates
#1

> **Predicate:** What the subject is or does.
>
> To find the predicate of any sentence, ask yourself, "What is the subject doing?" or "Is the subject something?"
>
> Example #1: The bird flew away.
>
> What did the bird do?   It "flew away"
>
> When the cat came around, the bird flew away.
>
> What did the bird do? It "flew away when the cat came around"
>
> Example #2: The children are happy.
>
> Are the children doing anything? No.
>
> Are the children something? Yes, they "are happy".
>
> **Remember:** If you see the words "is, are, was, were, or am", then the predicate is explaining what the subject IS.

Directions: 1. Circle the subject in each sentence. 2. Underline the predicate in each sentence. 3. Write "Is" on the line if the predicate explains what the subject is. Write "Does" if the predicate explains what the subject does.

Examples:

___Does___   The bird flew away when the cat came around.

___Does___   When the cat came around, the bird flew away.

Is or Does?   **(Be sure to ask, "What did the subject do?)**

___**Is**___ 1. Mrs. Garcia is my teacher at Elliot School.

_____ 2. At Elliot School, Mrs. Garcia is my teacher.

_____ 3. Our tree is bare in December.

_____ 4. In December our tree is bare.

_____ 5. After school, the teacher gave us a pencil.

_____ 6. The teacher gave us a pencil after school.

_____ 7. During recess, leaves were everywhere.

_____ 8. Leaves were everywhere during recess.

Predicates #2

```
Simple and Complete Predicates
```

The **predicate** tells what the subject is or does.

The **complete predicate** tells everything the subject is or does.

The **simple predicate** is the main verb or verb phrase that tells what the subject is or does.

Examples:

The dog is barking at the mailman.

Subject = dog   **Complete Predicate** = is barking at the mailman

Simple Predicate = is barking

Directions: Underline the complete predicate in each sentence. Circle the simple predicate. Write "Is" on the line if the predicate explains what the subject is. Write "Does" if the predicate explains what the subject does.

Example: __**Does**__   Amy dropped the penny into the fountain.

Is or Does?   **(Be sure to ask, "What did the subject do?")**

_____ 1. We made caramel apples.

_____ 2. I am sorry about the broken glass.

_____ 3. The magnet pulled the nails across the table.

_____ 4. A puppy is hungry.

_____ 5. Some puppies played on the grass.

_____ 6. The bell rang at the end of recess.

_____ 7. Those students were leaders of student council.

_____ 8. Many people are good helpers during the holidays.

_____ 9. We are good workers.

_____ 10. The drivers found a safe place to park during the storm.

Predicates
#3

Directions: Circle the simple predicate in each sentence. Underline the complete predicate. Write "Is" on the line if the predicate explains what the subject is. Write "Does" if the predicate explains what the subject does.

Example: __**Does**__ Amy (dropped) the penny into the fountain.

Is or Does?   (Be sure to ask, "What did the subject do?)

_____ 1. Emily rode the pony all morning.

_____ 2. She is an expert rider.

_____ 3. Our old car broke down.

_____ 4. We are happy about walking to school.

_____ 5. The big brown truck drove down the street.

_____ 6. The parents are happy with their children.

_____ 7. A lion is king of the jungle.

_____ 8. Some boys threw small, rubber spiders in our laps.

_____ 9. The show was ready to start.

_____ 10. A purple dinosaur sang a song about friends.

_____ 11. The girls are winners of the game.

_____ 12. The boys were good sports.

Extension: Write three (3) sentences using the predicate as an "is" and three sentences (3) using the predicate as a does. Use the three words below as your subjects.

puppies   kittens   sharks

Example:
"Is" – Puppies are cute.
"Does" - Puppies love to nibble on your ears.

Finding
Subjects and Predicates
#1

What is a subject? _____

What is a predicate? _____

I. If the complete subject is underlined, write "subject" on the line. If the complete predicate is underlined, write "predicate" on the line.

   Remember, ask yourself: "Who or what is the subject, and what did it do?"

__predicate__   1. After the rain, the clouds went away.

_____   2. The dark clouds came back the next day.

_____   3. Mary drank all of the milk.

_____   4. A big bottle of orange juice was still in the refrigerator.

_____   5. Dad gave a large red rose to Mom.

_____   6. A wet, sloppy kiss was planted on Dad's cheek.

_____   7. Our entire family worked on a puzzle all day.

_____   8. The silly puzzle took three hours to build.

_____   9. Before school we finished our homework.

_____   10. After recess our wonderful teacher gave us prizes.

II. Circle the simple subject and simple predicate in each sentence from Part I.

Finding
Subjects and Predicates
#2

I. If the complete subject is underlined, write "subject" on the line. If the complete predicate is underlined, write "predicate" on the line.

Remember, ask yourself: "Who or what is the subject, and what did it do?"

__**predicate**__   1. Before the concert the director gave a speech.

_____   2. A strong wind blew over our tent.

_____   3. Linda wore a beautiful, red sweater.

_____   4. A hungry lion chased that zebra.

_____   5. The shiny trophy on the table will be given today.

_____   6. The campers built a campfire.

_____   7. Several girls roasted marsh mellows.

_____   8. A little squirrel raced across the ground.

_____   9. At the lake the boys swung from tires into the water.

_____   10. After the concert the audience cheered loudly.

II. Circle the simple subject and simple predicate in each sentence in Part I.

Extension: Write five (5) sentences about a party. Circle the simple subject and simple predicate in each sentence.

Finding
Subjects and Predicates
#3

I. Finding the Subject and Predicate

Directions: Circle the simple subject. Underline the complete predicate.

Example: The (ball) rolled down the hill.
 What   Does

1. The frog jumped into the water.

2. The fish is in the pond.

3. Some big, hairy spiders live under that rock.

4. I am tired of washing the dog.

5. A fly buzzed around my ear.

6. A cow was in the field.

7. Mother bears protect their cubs.

8. Turtle eggs hatch in the sand.

9. Many birds are wet because of the rain.

10. The lizard's tail broke off.

11. The toucan is yellow and red with orange feathers.

12. Several butterflies are on the grass.

II. Subjects = Who or What / Predicates = Is or Does

Directions: Look at the sentences in Part I. Write "who" or "what" below each subject. Write "is" or "does" below each predicate.

117

Finding
Subjects and Predicates
#4

I. Finding the Subject and Predicate

    Directions: Circle the subject. Underline the complete predicate.

    Example: The (ball) rolled down the hill.
               What   Does

1. Cheetahs are faster than zebras.

2. The silver fish glistened in the light.

3. A snake rested on a rock in the warm sun.

4. The clever mouse always tricks the cat.

5. Some hungry kittens waited for their mother.

6. A scarecrow in the field scared away the birds.

7. The silly turkey wants to fly.

8. Several horses galloped across the field.

9. A bull dog is strong.

10. Worms are good diggers.

11. A little lizard climbed the wall.

12. That big, bad dog ate my homework.

II. Subjects = Who or What / Predicates = Is or Does

    Directions: Look at the sentences in Part I. Write "who" or "what"
                 below each subject. Write "is" or "does" below each predicate.

> **Extension:** Below is a list of subjects. Add a predicate to each subject
> by explaining what the subject IS. Use "is, are, was, or were."
>
>   1. The teachers   2. The students   3. The parents
>   4. The playground   5. The homework

Chapter 5
Review #1

I. Four Types of Sentences

Directions: Write Declarative, Interrogative, Exclamatory, or Imperative next to each sentence. Put a period, exclamation point, or question mark at the end.

_____ 1. We dressed as pirates for the party____

_____ 2. Where did you get that beautiful dress____

_____ 3. Set the book over there____

_____ 4. "There's a bee on your head____" shouted Mary.

_____ 5. Ask the teacher for a pencil____

_____ 6. How many times do we need to read the letter____

_____ 7. Mom screamed, "I just won the lottery____"

_____ 8. Some say that cats have nine lives____

II. Subjects and Predicates

A. Subjects: Who or What?

Directions: Is each subject below a who or a what? Write "who" or "what" next to each word.

_____ 1. snow   _____ 5. reporter

_____ 2. doctor   _____ 6. desk

_____ 3. soldier   _____ 7. cane

_____ 4. street   _____ 8. president

B. **Directions**: Underline the complete predicate in each sentence. Write "Is" on the line if the predicate explains what the subject is. Write "Does" if the predicate explains what the subject does.

Is or Does?   **(Be sure to ask, "What did the subject do?)**

_____ 1. The Trojans are the champions.

_____ 2. A river flows across my grandpa's farm.

_____ 3. During recess children played on the swings.

_____ 4. We were tired after the game.

_____ 5. Rain drops fell on our heads.

III. Finding the Subject and Predicate

Directions: Circle the simple subject. Underline the complete predicate.

Example: The (ball) rolled down the hill.

1. Some red paint spilled out of the cup.

2. Flowers are in the garden.

3. Bats hang from the top of caves.

4. My dog barked at the cat for an hour.

5. Our class is the best.

6. Spiders spin beautiful webs.

7. Cindy drank all of the juice.

8. She was late for dinner.

Chapter 5
Review #2

I. Four Types of Sentences

Directions: Write Declarative, Interrogative, Exclamatory, or Imperative next to each sentence. Put a period, exclamation point, or question mark at the end.

_____ 1. Will I get a good grade on this test____

_____ 2. Put your sweater in the closet____

_____ 3. Carrie shouted, "There's a spider in my hair____"

_____ 4. We're going to the dentist tomorrow____

_____ 5. A tornado is coming____

_____ 6. What is your favorite candy____

_____ 7. Chocolate is my favorite____

_____ 8. Don't eat that candy until after dinner____

II. Subjects and Predicates

A. Subjects: Who or What?

Directions: Is each subject below a who or a what? Write "who" or "what" next to each word.

_____ 1. secretary   _____ 5. stapler

_____ 2. hospital   _____ 6. leader

_____ 3. lady   _____ 7. director

_____ 4. bread   _____ 8. pocket

B. **Directions**: Underline the complete predicate in each sentence. Write "Is" on the line if the predicate explains what the subject is. Write "Does" if the predicate explains what the subject does.

Is or Does?   **(Be sure to ask, "What did the subject do?)**

_____ 1. Many birds fly south for the winter.

_____ 2. My mom is a teacher.

_____ 3. The puppies were ready for a bone.

_____ 4. Happy children threw darts at the balloons.

_____ 5. Ants find food in the weirdest places.

III. Finding the Subject and Predicate

Directions: Circle the simple subject. Underline the complete predicate.

Example: The (ball) rolled down the hill.

1. Butterflies are hard to catch.

2. Our class reads the most books every month.

3. Ken is a born leader.

4. Bright, colorful flowers grow in our garden.

5. A strange sound came from the corner of the room.

6. My new doll talks to me.

7. We are best friends.

8. A funny clown sprayed water in someone's face.

Unit 6

Phrases

Fragment and Run-On Sentences

Titles or Topic Sentences

Subject-Verb Agreement

Grammar Standards – Unit 6

_____
Student

	Mastery	Non-Mastery
1. Phrases		
2. Fragment and Run-On Sentences		
3. Title or Topic Sentence		
4. Subject-Verb Agreement		

Grammar Standards – Unit 6

_____
Student

	Mastery	Non-Mastery
1. Phrases		
2. Fragment and Run-On Sentences		
3. Title or Topic Sentence		
4. Subject-Verb Agreement		

Phrases #1

> A **sentence** tells a **complete thought**.
>
> A **phrase** is a **group of words** that <u>help</u> tell the complete thought. Some students think that they are writing sentences when they are just writing phrases.
>
> ### Two Types of Phrases
> 1. **Prepositional Phrase**: Begins with a preposition and ends with its object.
>   Examples: <u>into</u> the <u>street</u>   <u>inside</u> the <u>room</u>
>   Preposition Object   Preposition Object

I. Prepositional Phrases
   Directions: The box shows some common prepositions. Write a preposition on the line that would complete the phrase. Use each preposition only once.

above	at	between	inside	out	under
across	before	by	into	outside	until
after	behind	for	of	over	up
against	below	from	on	through	with
around	beside	in	onto	to	without

1. _____ the room

2. _____ the fence

3. _____ my shoe

4. _____ my shoe

5. _____ my shoe

6. _____ my shoe

7. _____ me

8. _____ the hill

9. _____ Joe

10. _____ you

11. _____ the trees

12. _____ school

13. _____ the cloud

14. _____ the cloud

15. _____ the cloud

16. _____ the cloud

17. _____ one o'clock

18. _____ a pencil

Extension: Write each preposition below in a phrase.

  above   **at**   **between**   **inside**   **out**
  under   **across**   **before**   **by**   **into**

Phrases
#2

A **sentence** tells a **complete thought**.

A **phrase** is a **group of words** that <u>help</u> tell the complete thought. Some students think that they are writing sentences when they are just writing phrases.

Two Types of Phrases

2. **Verb Phrase:** A group of words which includes the helping verbs and the main verb.

Examples: <u>is</u> <u>running</u>   <u>will be</u> <u>running</u>

              helping verb main verb   helping verbs main verb

---

I. Verb Phrases

Directions: The box shows some common helping verbs. Write a helping verb on the line that would complete the verb phrase. Use each helping verb only once.

Helping Verbs							
is	are	was	were	be	been	being	can
could	did	do	does	had	has	have	may
might	must	shall	should	will	would		

1. __**is**__ jumping

2. _____ smile

3. _____ climbed

4. _____ write

5. _____ been waiting

6. _____ be making

7. _____ walking

8. _____ have stopped

9. _____ sing

10. _____ call

11. _____ written

12. _____ make

Extension: Write five (5) sentences using any of the verb phrases from above.

Example: The car <u>should have stopped</u> at the light.

Phrases
#3

I. Directions: If the phrase below is a <u>prepositional phrase</u>, write "Prep" on the line. If the phrase is a <u>verb phrase</u>, write "Verb."

_____ 1. in the house

_____ 2. is swimming

_____ 3. without me

_____ 4. are jumping

_____ 5. through the cloud

_____ 6. inside the fence

_____ 7. will be drinking

_____ 8. for me

_____ 9. must play

_____ 10. did walk

II. Underline all of the phrases in each sentence. Below the phrase, write "Prep" if it is a prepositional phrase, "Verb" if it is a verb phrase.

1. A girl <u>is jumping</u> <u>on the trampoline</u>.   (2)
   Verb   **Prep**

2. At the movies the usher was giving toys to the children.   (3)

3. After school some students will be playing with their friends.   (3)

4. The coach is talking to his players inside the dugout.   (3)

5. Alicia has been reading a letter from her mom for an hour.   (3)

6. A ball has rolled against the fence.   (2)

7. Yolanda must be working really hard on her test.   (2)

8. In a month we will be taking a test on the body systems.   (3)

Extension: Write each preposition below in a phrase.

after	behind	for	of	over
up	against	below	from	on

Phrases
#4

I. Directions: If the phrase below is a prepositional phrase, write "Prep" on the line. If the phrase is a verb phrase, write "Verb."

_____ 1. from Dad   _____ 6. without any money

_____ 2. will be working   _____ 7. has thought

_____ 3. has been singing   _____ 8. during recess

_____ 4. beside the teacher   _____ 9. can read

_____ 5. does help   _____ 10. inside the box

II. Underline all the phrases in each sentence. Below the phrase, write "Prep" if it is a prepositional phrase, "Verb" if it is a verb phrase.

1. Some penguins <u>were diving</u> <u>into the water</u>.   (2)
   Verb   **Prep**

2. A funny looking bird with spiky hair was squawking at the children. (3)

3. At the mall a man in a clown suit was making animal balloons.   (3)

4. The children had played for five minutes at recess.   (3)

5. Mom does clean in my room every day.   (2)

6. Everyone in our class will be making a card for Valentine's Day.   (3)

7. The girl in the pink sweater is riding my bike.   (2)

8. Alma must be studying for her test at the library.   (3)

Extension: Write each verb phrase below in a sentence.

had played   **is riding**   **will be making**   **does clean**

Phrases
#5

Directions: Use any subject, prepositional phrase, and verb phrase from below to write sentences.

Subject	Verb Phrase	Prepositional Phrase
The dog	can run	across the sky
A cow	is walking	in the mud
Birds	will work	~~outside the fence~~
Mice	was chewing	around the barn
A plane	had slept	on a bone
Several ants	~~had escaped~~	outside my window
The farmer	were chirping	through a maze
The pigs	was flying	into the kitchen
~~Some chickens~~	might crawl	in the field

1. ___**Some chickens had escaped outside the fence.**_____

2. _____

3. _____

4. _____

5. _____

6. _____

7. _____

8. _____

9. _____

Fragment and Run-on Sentences
#1

A **sentence** tells a <u>complete thought</u>.

A **fragment** sentence does not tell a complete thought. It might be missing the subject (who? or what?) or the predicate (what the subject is or does).

A fragment missing the <u>subject</u> - Riding on his bike.

A fragment missing the <u>predicate</u> - The best game in the world.

Directions: If the sentence below is a fragment, write "fragment." If it is a complete thought, write "sentence."

_____ 1. Swinging back and forth on the swing.

_____ 2. We went down the slide head first.

_____ 3. The boys played basketball.

_____ 4. Crawling in the grass.

_____ 5. Ants all over our picnic table.

_____ 6. Dora had an adventure.

_____ 7. The ghost in the attic.

_____ 8. Dolphins live in the ocean.

_____ 9. The puppy will bark for a treat.

_____ 10. Making cookies with my sister.

Extension: There are five (5) fragment sentences on this worksheet.
Rewrite the fragment sentences by adding words to
complete the thought.

Fragment and Run-on Sentences
#2

A **sentence** tells a <u>complete thought</u>.
A **run-on** sentence has two or more complete thoughts.
Run-on: Kristy collects stuffed animals she keeps them on her bed.
Two Complete Thoughts: Kristy collects stuffed animals.
She keeps them on her bed.

Directions: Rewrite each run-on sentence below. Turn them into two complete sentences. You may need to add some words.

1. Mom made a dress for my party it was beautiful.

   _____

2. We went to the park then our teacher planted some flowers.

   _____

3. Toucans are beautiful birds they live in the jungle.

   _____

4. Crystal went on the swing she went very high.

   _____

5. Bobby made a sandcastle then he went into the water.

   _____

6. Our parrot is funny he can tell a knock-knock joke.

   _____

7. I played in the mud my Mom is going to be mad.

   _____

8. A button fell off of my shirt it landed in my soup.

   _____

Fragment and Run-on Sentences
#3

Directions: For each sentence below write F if the sentence is a fragment, RO if it is a run-on, and S if it is a complete sentence.

_____ 1. The phone rang.

_____ 2. The person on the phone.

_____ 3. We talked for hours it was nice.

_____ 4. Played in the sand.

_____ 5. A wave came it knocked over our castle.

_____ 6. My brother laughed at our wet castle.

_____ 7. The girls ran to the playground they played tetherball.

_____ 8. Gloria was the first to win a game.

_____ 9. Swinging as hard as she could.

_____ 10. The lion is the king of the jungle.

_____ 11. A lion with big ferocious teeth.

_____ 12. The lion roared all the animals ran.

Extension: There are four (4) fragment sentences on this worksheet. Rewrite the fragment sentences by adding words to complete the thought.

Name: _____

Fragment and Run-on Sentences
#4

Directions: For each sentence below write F if the sentence is a fragment, RO if it is a run-on, and S if it is a complete sentence.

_____ 1. The best carnival in the world.

_____ 2. John won a prize at the carnival.

_____ 3. He threw the ball the milk bottles crashed.

_____ 4. Our family went to the game.

_____ 5. Cheering for our favorite team.

_____ 6. A horn blew we all yelled.

_____ 7. Coach let me be goalie I stopped three shots.

_____ 8. Diving across the grass to stop the ball.

_____ 9. Jose is a great soccer player.

_____ 10. Sledding head first down the hill.

_____ 11. It snowed all night then we played all day.

_____ 12. We raced down the hill on our sleds.

Extension: Fix all of the run-on sentences from this worksheet.

Fragment and Run-on Sentences
#5

Directions: The story below is one giant run-on sentence.
1. Circle every "and" and "then".
2. Rewrite the story. Replace every "and" and "then" with a period. Capitalize the next word.

I had the best birthday party ever and all of my friends were there and we hit a piñata then we played games in our back yard then we ate ice cream with any topping we wanted and then I got to open my presents and it was the greatest party ever.

Rewrite the story:

_____

_____

_____

_____

_____

_____

_____

Titles or
Topic Sentences #1

Topic Sentence:

In a paragraph, the topic sentence tells the main idea of the paragraph. Many young writers confuse a title with a topic sentence. What is wrong with the topic sentence below?

The most exciting day of my life.

This would make a good title, but it is a fragment sentence. The box below explains how to make a title. Use these rules to write good titles. However, make sure your topic sentences make a complete thought.

Titles
1. Capitalize the first, last, and all the important words.
2. Do not capitalize A, An, The, and prepositions that are less than 5 letters unless they are the first or last word of the title.
3. Capitalize prepositions that are 5 words or more.

Examples: **The Longest Day of the Year** / **Hope Without Fear**

Directions: Are the statements below titles or topic sentences? Write "sentence" if the statement is a sentence. If it is a title, rewrite it by using the rules of capitalization.

1. The longest day of the year. _____The Longest Day of the Year_____

2. Spot is a funny dog. _____

3. Hope without fear. _____

4. My favorite toy. _____

5. The biggest tree house in the world. _____

6. You'll never believe what I did yesterday. _____

7. Singing a song in the chorus. _____

8. America is the best country in the world. _____

135

Titles or
Topic Sentences #2

Directions: For each statement below, write "title" if it is a title. Write "sentence" if it is a sentence.

_____ 1. The longest day of the year.

_____ 2. It was the longest day of the year.

_____ 3. We took the long way home.

_____ 4. The long way home.

_____ 5. Three wishes for everyone.

_____ 6. The genie gave three wishes.

_____ 7. I wrote a letter for my teacher.

_____ 8. A letter for my teacher.

_____ 9. Sean had a surprise party.

_____ 10. A surprise party for Sean.

_____ 11. The Fourth of July picnic.

_____ 12. Our family had a picnic on the Fourth of July.

_____ 13. Attack of the hungry squirrels.

_____ 14. The camp was attacked by hungry squirrels.

_____ 15. Great topic sentences.

Extension: You know that titles need to have all the important words capitalized. In the worksheet above, there are eight (8) titles. Rewrite all the titles from above so that all the important words are capitalized.

Remember to capitalize the first, last, and all the important words. A, An, The, and all prepositions that are five letters or less should not be capitalized unless they are the first or last words.

Example: The black cat.   The **Black Cat**

Titles or
Topic Sentences #3

Directions: For each statement below, write "title" if it is a title. Write "sentence" if it is a sentence.

_____ 1. The best pizza in the world.

_____ 2. My mouth had a party.

_____ 3. The day of the big race.

_____ 4. It was the day of the big race.

_____ 5. Tammy and I are best friends.

_____ 6. Best friends forever.

_____ 7. Wrestling in the dirt.

_____ 8. The boys were wrestling in the dirt.

_____ 9. I taught Fido silly dog tricks.

_____ 10. Silly dog tricks.

_____ 11. It rained like crazy today.

_____ 12. Rain from the sky.

_____ 13. My dad played a funny joke on me.

_____ 14. Funny joke by my dad.

_____ 15. Complete thoughts for topic sentences.

Extension: Rewrite all eight (8) of the titles from above. Follow the rules for capitalizing titles. Use the space below the titles.

Subject-Verb Agreement
#1

Name: _____

What is wrong with the sentences below?

#1 Andre ride his skateboard very well.

#2 Brian and Tom is my best friends.

These sentences break the **subject-verb agreement** rule. If the subject of the sentence is singular (one thing), the verb must be singular. If the subject in the sentence is plural (more than one thing), the verb must be plural.

What is the subject of sentence #1? Andre (Singular)

What is the verb of sentence #1? ride (Plural)

Singular verbs need an "s" or "es".   Andre <u>rides</u> his skateboard very well.

Plural verbs do not have an "s".   They <u>ride</u> their skateboards very well.

Other singular verbs: "is" and "was"
Other plural verbs: "are" and "were"

Brian and Tom <u>are</u> my best friends.
Tom <u>is</u> my best friend.

Directions: Are the subjects below singular or plural? 1. Underline the subject in each sentence. 2. Below the subjects write S if it is singular or P if it is plural. 3. Circle the verb that fits the sentence.

1. <u>Omar</u> (buy , (buys)) a new video game every year.
   S

2. Several large, hairy spiders (make , makes) webs in our yard.

3. The girls on the bench (is , are) doing their homework.

4. The water in the buckets (is , are) very dirty so don't drink it.

5. Many hungry customers (order , orders) large meals.

6. My dad (watch , watches) football every Sunday.

7. The boys on the bed (play , plays) rough.

8. Our team (was , were) ready to play.

138

Subject-Verb Agreement
#2

I. Are the subjects below singular or plural? 1. Underline the subject in each sentence. 2. Below the subjects write S if it is singular or P if it is plural. 3. Circle the verb that fits the sentence.

1. The children (eat , eats) very quickly.

2. Our teacher (is , are) getting ready for our test.

3. Babies in the nursery (climb , climbs) all over the toys.

4. Every December Chris (write , writes) a letter to Santa.

5. Thomas, using his colored pencils, (draw , draws) amazing pictures.

6. We (is , are) going to the library today.

7. The people in the village always (wash , washes) in the river.

8. When students finish their drawings, they (color , colors) the pictures.

9. The dress with the pretty flowers (was , were) beautiful.

10. Players in the game (throw , throws) beanbags on the squares.

II. Write C on the line if each sentence below has a correct subject and verb. Write I if it is incorrect. If incorrect, then change the verb to make it correct.

__I__ 1. Amy ~~read~~ every night before she goes to bed.
       reads
_____ 2. The cowboys rides their horses.

_____ 3. At the rodeo a clown chase the bull to protect the bull riders.

_____ 4. The dancers in the parade wear beautiful costumes.

_____ 5. Whenever we have pizza my dog bark until he gets a bite.

_____ 6. The man with the guitar plays very well.

Subject-Verb Agreement
#3

I. Are the subjects below singular or plural? 1. Underline the subject in each sentence. 2. Below the subjects write S if it is singular or P if it is plural. 3. Circle the verb that fits the sentence.

1. The jet (fly , flys) quickly across the sky.

2. Doctors at the hospital (was , were) ready to help.

3. Every day the coaches (teach , teaches) us a new skill.

4. If the boys with the telescope (look, looks) closely, they can see the planet.

5. Many people (think , thinks) that writing is fun.

6. The reporters said that our school (is , are) the best.

7. The president of the soccer leagues (feel , feels) we are doing well.

8. When she (touch , touches) the turtle's head, it hides in its shell.

II. Write C on the line if each sentence below has a correct subject and verb. Write I if it is incorrect. If incorrect, then change the verb to make it correct.

_____ 1. Many cars races around the track very quickly.

_____ 2. Mrs. Smith always shows us better ways to study.

_____ 3. During the slumber party the girls hits each other with pillows.

_____ 4. Dad tell ghost stories and scare us a lot.

_____ 5. My brothers play with their remote control cars all the time.

_____ 6. Our choir sing five songs at every show.

Extension: Write each verb below in a sentence. Underline your subject in each sentence. Write "singular" or "plural" below it.

plays   read   are   cuts   talk

Example: <u>Mary</u> **plays** with her dolls.
Singular

Subject-Verb Agreement
#4

Name: _____

I. **Directions**: Write a verb on the line in each sentence that fits the subject-verb rule. Keep all of the verbs in the <u>present</u> tense.

1. Every day a man _____ past our house.

2. We all _____ our new folders.

3. Every time my dad jogs he _____ a lot of water.

4. Babies don't know how to talk so they _____ to get what they want.

5. Jenny _____ her stuffed animals when she is happy.

6. If you _____ a good story, you will get a good grade.

7. The children _____ a lot during recess.

8. He always _____ when it rains.

II. Below is a story. As you read it you will notice that the subject-verb agreement rule has been broken many times. Each time the rule is broken, cross out the verb and rewrite it in the space below.

Every day when I ~~walks~~ home from school, a big black dog chase me down my
               walk

block. It see me coming when I turn the corner. My sister run the other way, but I

choose to face it. I stands firm with my fists high in the air and I yells, "Aaaahhhh."

Dogs hates when you do that. They thinks you are big and powerful so they runs

away. My sister are too afraid to try it. I don't blames her. Sometimes when I tries

it, some dogs knocks me over. I guess it would be safer for us if we takes another way

home. It are not good to mess with strange dogs.

Did you find all 14?

Chapter 6
Review

I. Phrases

Directions: Underline all the phrases in each sentence. Below the phrase, write "Prep" if it is a prepositional phrase or "Verb" if it is a verb phrase.

1. A girl <u>is jumping</u> <u>on the trampoline</u>.   (2)
               Verb   Prep

2. Before the game the coach was talking to the players.   (3)

3. After lunch some students were playing in the sandbox.   (3)

4. Mom is making cookies in the kitchen.   (2)

5. Amy will be walking to school.   (2)

6. The puppy in the corner is sleeping on its new bed.   (3)

II. Fragment and Run-On Sentences

Directions: For each sentence below write F if the sentence is a fragment, RO if it is a run-on, and S if it is a complete sentence.

_____   1. The dog barked.

_____   2. The dog in the yard.

_____   3. We pet the puppy it was nice.

_____   4. Making cookies in the kitchen.

_____   5. Mom poured the mix I stirred it.

_____   6. The cookies tasted great.

_____   7. I read a good book.

_____   8. The book was funny I read it again.

_____   9. The best book I ever read.

III. Title or Topic Sentence

Directions: For each statement below, write "title" if it is a title. Write "sentence" if it is a sentence.

_____ 1. The happiest day of my life.

_____ 2. It was the happiest day of my life.

_____ 3. I was drawing a picture for Mom.

_____ 4. Drawing a picture for Mom.

_____ 5. Free ice cream for everyone.

IV. Subject-Verb Agreement

Directions: Write C on the line if each sentence below has a correct subject and verb. Write I if it is incorrect. If incorrect, then change the verb to make it correct.

_____ 1. My dad drive to work every day.

_____ 2. The bunnies hop all around the yard.

_____ 3. The singers is ready to go.

_____ 4. The girls in the car fix their hair.

_____ 5. While the band plays, the players practices their drills.

Unit 7

Homonyms

Compound Words

A vs. An

Student

	Mastery	Non-Mastery
1. Homonyms		
2. Compound Words		
3. A vs. An		

Homonyms
Group #1

Homonyms (homophones) are words that sound the same but are different in spelling or meaning.

In the box below are five (5) groups of homonyms. Use these worksheets to learn the differences between the words.

Homonyms
Group #1

there – tells about a place	Example: Put the book <u>there</u>.
their – belonging to someone	Example: This is <u>their</u> room.
they're – contraction for "they are"	Example: <u>They're</u> nice.
no – a negative response	Example: <u>No</u>, you cant' go.
know – to understand something	Example: I <u>know</u> how to swim.
to – connecting word.	Example: We went <u>to</u> school.
two – the number 2	Example: We have <u>two</u> eyes.
too – also or extreme amount	Example: He's <u>too</u> young <u>too</u>.
won – past tense of win	Example: They <u>won</u> the game.
one – the number 1	Example: I have <u>one</u> nose.
son – parents male child	Example: He looks like his <u>son</u>.
sun – the star in the center of our solar system	Example: The <u>sun</u> is bright.

Study the Homonyms

Make study pictures for each homonym. A study picture is a way of tricking yourself into remembering the differences between the two (or three) words.

Example: Sun has a "u" / Son has an "o". Draw a sun in the shape of a "U".

Sun	Son

Homonyms

<table>
<tr><td colspan="3">Homonyms - Group #1</td></tr>
<tr><td>there, their, they're</td><td>no, know</td><td>to, two, too,</td></tr>
<tr><td>won, one,</td><td colspan="2">sun, son</td></tr>
</table>

I. On a separate sheet of paper, write each homonym from Group #1 in a sentence.

II. Read your sentences to a partner. Ask them to spell the homonym from each of your sentences.

III. Fill in the blanks with a word from Homonym Group #1.

1. _____ going to be late tonight.

2. He threw the ball _____ me.

3. The dad and his _____ will be on the same team.

4. Mom said _____ but Dad said yes.

5. We went to _____ house to do our homework.

6. The Angels played hard and _____ the game.

7. Everyone has _____ eyes and one mouth.

8. Put the box over _____.

9. After the rain the _____ finally came out.

10. The field was _____ wet for us to play today.

11. If you multiply any number by _____ the answer will be itself.

12. We all _____ how to multiply by five.

Homonyms
Group #1 - Practice

Homonyms - Group #1
there, their, they're   no, know   to, two, too,
won, one,   sun, son

Directions: Fill in the blanks with a word from Homonym Group #1.

1. We _____ someone who can fix your bike.

2. Jennifer kicked a goal, and we _____ the game.

3. The light from the _____ is bright today.

4. It was _____ windy to go on the rides.

5. _____ is a big spider on the sink.

6. There was only _____ donut left so I let him have it.

7. The class put _____ backpacks against the wall.

8. After dinner I wasn't hungry so I said _____ to dessert.

9. I always have two pencils in case _____ breaks.

10. They walked all the way _____ the store.

11. _____ the best players on the team.

12. John is his dad's oldest _____.

Extension: Write the following homonyms in a sentence:
there   their   know   too   son

149

Homonyms
Group #2

Homonyms (homophones) are words that sound the same but are different in spelling or meaning.

In the box below are five (5) groups of homonyms. Use these worksheets to learn the differences between the words.

Homonyms
Group #2

steal – taking what is not yours	Example: Don't <u>steal</u>.
steel – strong iron alloy	Example: It's as strong as <u>steal</u>.
ate – past tense of eat	Example: She <u>ate</u> the pizza.
eight – the number 8	Example: A squid has <u>eight</u> arms.
blue – the color blue / sad	Example: She felt <u>blue</u> yesterday.
blew – past tense of blow	Example: The wind <u>blew</u> all day.
here – this place	Example: Put the book <u>here</u>.
hear – able to take in sound	Example: Can you <u>hear</u> me?
close – to shut	Example: Don't <u>close</u> the door.
clothes – garments that cover the body	Example: Wash your <u>clothes</u>.

Study the Homonyms

Make study pictures for each homonym. A study picture is a way of tricking yourself into remembering the differences between the two (or three) words.

Example: Blue is a color and means sad.   Blew has a "w" just like "wind".

Blue	**Blew**
	Blew
	i
	n
	d
She is blue and cries blue tears.	

Homonyms

Homonyms - Group #2
steal, steel   ate, eight   blue, blew
here, hear   close, clothes

I. On a separate sheet of paper, write each homonym from Group #2 in a sentence.

II. Read your sentences to a partner. Ask them to spell the homonym from each of your sentences.

III. Fill in the blanks with a word from Homonym Group #2.

1. The wind _____ hard for over an hour.

2. If you _____ you might go to jail.

3. An octopus has _____ legs called tentacles.

4. We all received new _____ for our birthdays.

5. The noise made it hard for us to _____ the television.

6. Don't forget to _____ the door.

7. Who _____ all of the pizza?

8. I love when there are no clouds and the sky is _____.

9. The building made of _____ is stronger than the one made of bricks.

10. The teacher told us to wait _____.

11. Rover _____ all of our hotdogs.

12. She fell into a puddle and got her _____ all wet.

Homonyms
Group #2 - Practice

Homonyms - Group #2
steal, steel   ate, eight   blue, blew
here, hear   close, clothes

Directions: Fill in the blanks with a word from Homonym Group #2.

1. I can't believe that my dog _____ my shoe.

2. Turn up the television so we can _____ better.

3. It was cold because Tim didn't _____ the door.

4. _____ paint and yellow paint will make green paint.

5. My dog buried my shoe right _____.

6. Our teacher always wears nice _____.

7. Dad _____ out the candles on his cake.

8. Maria swam _____ laps in the pool.

9. If you listen carefully you will _____ the ocean.

10. Bank robbers tried to _____ the money.

11. The wind _____ all night and knocked over the trees.

12. The bank robbers were locked behind _____ bars.

Extension: Write the following homonyms in a sentence:

steal   clothes   close   hear   here

Homonyms
Group #3

Homonyms (homophones) are words that sound the same but are different in spelling or meaning.

In the box below are five (5) groups of homonyms. Use these worksheets to learn the differences between the words.

Homonyms
Group #3

weigh – to measure something's weight	Example: How much do you <u>weigh</u>?
way – direction / how to do something	Example: Go this way. Do it the right <u>way</u>.
week – seven days	Example: We'll be here for a <u>week</u>.
weak – not much strength	Example: The heat made us <u>weak</u>.
I'll – contraction for "I will"	Example: <u>I'll</u> be ready.
aisle – path between seats	Example: Walk down the <u>aisle</u>.
isle – small island	Example: The <u>isle</u> was beautiful.
threw – past tense of throw	Example: He <u>threw</u> the ball.
through – traveling across the middle of	Example: The plane went <u>through</u> the clouds.
flew – past tense of fly	Example: The bird <u>flew</u> away.
flu – sickness, short for influenza	Example: She had the <u>flu</u>.

Study the Homonyms

Make study pictures for each homonym. A study picture is a way of tricking yourself into remembering the differences between the two (or three) words.

Example: Flew and wind have a "W"   You "U" have the flu.

Flew
Flew
i
n
d
The birds flew through the wind.

Flu

Homonyms

Homonyms - Group #3
weigh, way   week, weak   I'll, aisle, isle
threw, through   flew, flu

I. On a separate sheet of paper, write each homonym from Group #3 in a sentence.

II. Read your sentences to a partner. Ask them to spell the homonym in each sentence.

III. Fill in the blanks with a word from Homonym Group #1.

1. In one _____ it will be summer vacation.

2. A bird _____ into the house.

3. The usher walked down the _____ with us.

4. The doctor will _____ you on his scale at his office.

5. The boat crashed on an _____ in the middle of the ocean.

6. Jimmy _____ the ball over the fence.

7. He was sick so he was too _____ to go to school.

8. Too many people are sick with the _____.

9. Do you know the _____ to Grandmother's house?

10. _____ study hard for my test.

11. A car crashed _____ a wall.

12. On the bus, would you like a window seat or an _____ seat?

Homonyms
Group #3 - Practice

Name: _____

Homonyms - Group #3
weigh, way   week, weak   I'll, aisle, isle threw, through   flew, flu

Directions: Fill in the blanks with a word from Homonym Group #3.

1. The store will _____ the candy which costs $2.25 a pound.

2. We had to walk home _____ the rain.

3. The chair broke because it was too _____.

4. _____ ask if you can sleep over tonight.

5. We all got a _____ shot so we wouldn't get sick.

6. The ship sailed out to a small _____ in the ocean.

7. He _____ his trash into the garbage.

8. Lee _____ his kite very high at the park.

9. The bride walked down the center _____ at the wedding.

10. She does everything the right _____.

11. Our family spent a _____ at the lake.

12. I ate healthy so I _____ less than I did last month.

Extension: Write the following homonyms in a sentence: **weigh**   **weak**   **aisle**   **threw**   **flu**

Homonyms
Review
#1

Group #1: there, their, they're, no, know, to, two, too, won, one, sun, son
Group #2: steal, steel, ate, eight, blue, blew, here, hear, close, clothes
Group #3: weight, way, week, weak, I'll, aisle, isle, threw, through, flew, flu

Directions: Fill in the blanks with a word from Homonym Groups #1, #2, or #3.

1. Do you want one sandwich or _____?

2. The American flag is red, white, and _____.

3. Do you _____ how to ride a bike?

4. _____ is much stronger than wood.

5. Yesterday he put his book on the table, but today it wasn't _____.

6. _____ the window so flies can't come in.

7. Bob and his _____ work together at the store.

8. My muscles are too _____ to lift these weights.

9. Mom went _____ the store.

10. When I ask my dad if I can play with his glasses he says _____.

11. Cameras are ready to catch anyone who might _____ something.

12. The wolf huffed and puffed and _____ his house down.

13. _____ not ready to start the game.

14. On Sunday we put on our best _____ for the party.

15. Spring break only lasts for a _____.

16. The boat stopped at a small _____ in the ocean.

Homonyms
Review
#2

Name: _____

Group #1:	there, their, they're, no, know, to, two, too, won, one, sun, son
Group #2:	steal, steel, ate, eight, blue, blew, here, hear, close, clothes
Group #3:	weigh, way, week, weak, I'll, aisle, isle, threw, through, flew, flu

Directions: Fill in the blanks with a word from Homonym Groups #1, #2, or #3.

1. When we got home it was _____ late to watch television.

2. We _____ a lot of pizza at the party.

3. Did you _____ that loud explosion?

4. They covered _____ books to keep them protected.

5. The bus driver can't find his _____ to the camp.

6. Our team was excited because we _____ the game.

7. _____ be ready in two minutes.

8. The quarterback _____ a pass to the receiver.

9. An octagon has _____ sides.

10. Wait _____, and I'll be back in a minute.

11. Step on the scale to see how much you _____.

12. Only _____ person at a time can play.

13. He put on dark glasses because the _____ was so bright.

14. The children ran _____ the puddle.

15. My seats are right on the _____ near the usher.

16. The plane _____ right over our heads.

157

Compound Words
#1

Compound means "made from two or more things".

A **compound word** is a word made by putting two words together.

Examples: hot + dog = hotdog   dog + house = doghouse

I. Combine the words below to form compound words.

1. every + body

_____

2. hand + shake

_____

3. card + board

_____

4. snow + ball

_____

5. rain + drop

_____

6. mail + box

_____

7. pop + corn

_____

8. blue + berry

_____

9. sail + boat

_____

10. eye + sight

_____

II. Make compound words by taking a word from Box A and putting it with Box B.

Box A		
~~news~~	chalk	air
waste	water	sea
thunder	snow	quick

Box B		
board	plane	storm
basket	proof	flake
sand	shore	~~paper~~

1. __**newspaper**__

2. _____

3. _____

4. _____

5. _____

6. _____

7. _____

8. _____

9. _____

158

Compound Words
#2

Name: _____

I. Combine the words below to form compound words.

    1. side + walk   4. trash + can

       _____   _____

    2. meat + ball   5. flash + light

       _____   _____

    3. drive + way   6. key + chain

       _____   _____

II. Underline the compound word in each sentence. Write the two words that form the compound word on the lines.

    1. She has posters all over her bedroom walls. _____ _____

    2. Amy drew hearts all over her notebook.   _____ _____

    3. The sidewalk has several cracks.   _____ _____

    4. The car went up the driveway.   _____ _____

    5. My birthday is in two weeks.   _____ _____

    6. He's the best shortstop on the team.   _____ _____

    7. John threw a baseball through a window. _____ _____

    8. The toy was on top of the bookshelf.   _____ _____

    9. Spaghetti tastes good with a meatball.   _____ _____

   10. Dad gets a paycheck every two weeks.   _____ _____

Extension: Select any five (5) compound words from this page. Write each one in a sentence.

Compound Words
#3

boy	space	tooth	finger
friend	ship	brush	nail
skate	land	under	race
board	slide	ground	horse
sea	water	class	melon
gull	fall	color	paper
super	eye	every	sand
market	sight	body	castle
life	earth	home	room
guard	quake	work	bed

I. Use the words in the box to form compound words. Write at least twenty compound words on the lines below. You may use a word from the box more than once.

_____

_____

_____

_____

_____

_____

II. Underline the compound word in each sentence. Write the two words that form the compound word on the lines.

1. We went to police headquarters.　　　_____ _____

2. The trashcan was full of garbage.　　　_____ _____

3. Mom eats oatmeal every morning.　　　_____ _____

4. The flashlight needs new batteries.　　　_____ _____

5. I need a keychain for my keys.　　　_____ _____

160

A vs. An
#1

A vs. An

Use "a" when the next word starts with a consonant.
Examples: **a** <u>b</u>all , **a** <u>h</u>at, **a** <u>d</u>og, **a** <u>f</u>ish, **a** <u>z</u>ebra

Use "an" when the next word starts with a vowel or vowel sound.
Examples: **an** <u>a</u>pple , **an** <u>e</u>agle, **an** <u>i</u>ceberg,
an <u>o</u>live, **an** <u>u</u>mbrella **an** <u>h</u>onor

I. Write five (5) words that would follow "a". Next, write five (5) words that would follow "an".

A	**An**
Example: a cat	Example: an egg

_____	_____
_____	_____
_____	_____
_____	_____
_____	_____

II. Fill in each blank with "a" or "an".

1. We saw _____ eagle flying past _____ nest.

2. Is _____ aardvark also called _____ anteater?

3. The teacher asked _____ question, but I didn't have _____ answer.

4. _____ car had _____ accident about _____ hour ago.

5. Tom wants to be _____ actor or _____ lawyer.

6. _____ guide will lead us on _____ adventure through the woods.

7. Will _____ airbag protect _____ passenger in _____ crash?

8. _____ crocodile looks a lot like _____ alligator.

A vs. An
#2

I. Fill in each blank with "a" or "an".

1. There was ____ Canadian, ____ American, and ____ Asian on the plane.

2. ____ aluminum can should be recycled.

3. Jennifer was ____ actress who played ____ angel in the play.

4. If there is ____ ant on ____ picnic blanket, there will soon be more ants.

5. At the zoo we saw ____ zebra, ____ monkey, and ____ elephant.

6. ____ apple would be ____ good snack at recess.

7. Do you live in ____ house or ____ apartment?

8. ____ manager asked him to fill out ____ application.

9. We have ____ orange tree, but I really want ____ avocado tree.

10. ____ Eskimo might catch ____ fish and live in ____ igloo.

II. You are on a nature hike. Write a story about things you see and do. Use "an" and "a" at least five times.

_____

_____

_____

_____

_____

_____

_____

_____

A vs. An
#3

I. Fill in each blank with "a" or "an".

1. _____ ice cream truck came by so I bought _____ popsicle.

2. We need _____ umbrella or _____ hood for our jackets.

3. It will take _____ army of people to make _____ new bridge.

4. _____ artist drew _____ picture of _____ sunset.

5. _____ office at our school has _____ letter for you.

6. For breakfast I had _____ pancake, _____ sausage, and _____ egg.

7. I think _____ armadillo has a shell to protect it from _____ predator.

8. They need _____ umpire for _____ baseball game.

9. _____ student wrote _____ article about _____ field trip.

10. _____ tree fell so we chopped it up with _____ ax.

II. You are grocery shopping with your mom. Write about the things you see, do, and buy in the store. Use "an" and "a" at least five times.

_____

_____

_____

_____

_____

_____

_____

_____

Unit 8

Friendly Letters

Grammar Standards – Unit 8

_____

Student

	Mastery	Non-Mastery
1. Friendly Letters		

Friendly Letters
#1

Below are two samples of how a friendly letter should look.

Heading Greeting, Body Closing, Signature	1685 Main St. Downy, CA 90715 January 1, 2005 Dear Jennifer, Guess what happened to me yesterday. I was at the mall. There was a booth set up for free make-overs. I got in line, and after an hour, it was my turn. The people there took my picture. They liked the picture so much that they're going to put it in a magazine. How exciting. I wonder what they meant by "a great 'before' picture". Write me back soon. Sincerely, Erika

Notice the following:

1. The heading, closing, and signature all line up on the right.

2. There is a comma after the greeting and the closing.

3. The first paragraph of the body is indented. You follow all the rules of writing.

Your assignment:

Copy the "Dear Jennifer" letter from above on a separate sheet of paper.

Make sure that the heading, closing, and signature are all lined up.

Friendly Letters
#2

Headings

The heading of a friendly letter looks like this:

Address	555 Elm St.
City, State, Zip Code	Redding, CA 91343
Date	April 7, 2006

Directions: Put the headings from each box in the correct order. Write each one on the lines to the right.

1.

> 314 Clarke Ave.
> December 15, 2000
> Downey, CA 90801

_____
_____
_____

2.

> 5063 Fallin Ave.
> Torrence, CA 90703
> March 10, 2008

_____
_____
_____

3.

> July 4, 1976
> Philadelphia, PA 19103
> 333 Market Street

_____
_____
_____

4.

> April 1, 2010
> Phoenix, AZ 70812
> 333 Desert Rd.

_____
_____
_____

Extension: Select any two of the headings from above. Write them on a separate sheet of paper as if you were writing a real letter.

Friendly Letters
#3

Below are two (2) one-sentence letters. Write them on the lines.   Be sure the heading, closing, and signature all line up on the right. Put a comma after the greeting and the closing.

#1

> 5895 Ball Street   /   Lakewood, CA 90715   / January 1, 2004   / Dear Alice,
> Be sure to indent your paragraphs in the body of a letter. In this way you will have a good looking letter.   /   Yours truly,   /   Cindi Rella

_____
_____
_____

_____ ,

_____
_____
_____

_____
_____

#2

> I got a bike today. What did you get? / 314 Main Street / Dear Mary, /
> Sincerely, / Joseph / Seal Beach, CA 90801 /   December 25, 2000

_____
_____
_____

_____ ,

_____
_____
_____

_____
_____

Friendly Letters
#4

Directions: On a separate sheet of paper, rewrite the letters below. Be sure to put them in the proper order.

#1

July 4, 1776   /   333 Market Street   /   Philadelphia, Pennsylvania 19103   /

Do you still have my pen?   /   Sincerely,   /   Dear George,   /   Thomas

#2

May 12, 1863   /   284 Black Forest Lane   /   Torrance, CA 90503   /   Gretel   /

I ran out of bread crumbs. The nice lady in a house made of candy has some.

Meet us in the forest.   /   Your sister,   /   Dear Hansel,

#3

Dear Alex,   /   Thanks for the present. The poster will look great in my room. /

Bobby   /   2290 Foxhill Ave.   /   Sincerely,   /   October 12, 2004   /

Arlington, TX 76014

#4

My family will be leaving for Orlando, Florida tomorrow. We're going to visit

Disneyworld. I'll send you a postcard.   /   August 2, 2005   /   Dear Kelly,   /

258 Berry Street   /   Sacramento, CA 89581   /   Yours truly,   /   Pat Smith

#5

Harry   /   Sincerely,   /   I left my flying broom back in the closet . If you send

it to me here in America, I'll bring you some magic candy next summer.   /

Dear Dudley, / September 13, 2002 / New York, NY 10128 / 333 Castle Dr.

Friendly Letters
#5

Directions: On a separate sheet of paper, rewrite the letters below. Be sure to put them in the proper order.

#1

April 1, 2008   /   911 Beach Blvd.   /   Seattle, WA 98103   /   I'm staying here at camp for two more weeks. April Fools! See you on Saturday   /   Your son,   /   Dear Mom,   /   Ryan

#2

June 14, 1856   /   487 Jungle Rd.   /   Miami, FL 33125   /   Jane   /   Thank you for the lovely time in your jungle. I loved your tree house.   Say hello to your animal friends.   /   Your friend,   /   Dear Tarzan,

#3

Dear Freddy,   /   How was your Christmas? Mine was great. I got a new bike and a new video game.   /   Billy   /   8544 Sugar Street   /   Sincerely,   /   December 25, 2004   /   Reno, NV 89502

#4

My family and I got to see the Space Shuttle land today. It was so exciting. We'll be in Yosemite tomorrow.   /   September 2, 2005   /   Dear Kyle,   /   912 Oak Ave.   /   Redding, CA 96003   /   Yours truly,   /   Michael Jones

#5

Marsha   /   Love,   /   Remember when you broke Mom's lamp? She always said not to play ball in the house.   /   Dear Peter,   /   May 30, 1972   /   Hollywood, CA 90068   /   621 Brady Lane

Extension: Write a letter to a friend. Be sure to use the correct format for letter writing.

Unit 9

Prefixes and Suffixes

Student

	Mastery	Non-Mastery
1. Prefixes		
2. Suffixes		

Prefixes
#1

> **Main Idea**: A prefix changes the **meaning** of a word.
>
> A prefix is a syllable added to **a base word** to change its meaning.
>
> Example: "**un**" means not. **un** + happy = not happy

I. Below are prefixes and their definitions. Add the prefix to the base word.
Next, use the prefix to <u>guess the definition</u> of the <u>new word</u>. Use a
dictionary to check your answers.

	Base Word	New Word	New Definition
1. re = again			
	write -	_____	- __to write again_____
			_____
	paint -	_____	- _____
			_____
	take -	_____	- _____
2. un = not			
	fair -	_____	- _____
			_____
	able -	_____	- _____
			_____
	selfish -	_____	- _____
3. pre = before			
	test -	_____	- _____
			_____
	school -	_____	- _____
			_____
	pay -	_____	- _____

> **Extension:** Select one word from each prefix above. Write each one in
> a sentence. Underline the prefix.

Prefixes
#2

I. Select a word from the box to complete each sentence.

1. Mom doesn't like the color so we need to _____ the house.	rewrite
2. Cindy thought getting a D on the test was _____.	repaint
3. Before going to kindergarten, I went to _____.	retake
4. If you are _____ you will share your crayons.	unfair
5. We revised our stories, and then we had to _____ them.	unable
6. The photographer had to _____ the picture.	unselfish
7. The new book comes out next year, but I can _____ now.	pretest
8. On Monday we take a spelling _____ before Friday's test.	preschool
9. If you're _____ to finish the math, ask for help.	prepay

II. Use a dictionary to look up two (2) words with the prefixes listed below. Write the **base word** on the line. Next, write the **base word** with the prefix together. Finally, write the definition of the word.

Note: When looking up the word, if there is no **base** word, it is not a prefix.

1. re – to do again   **2. un = not**   **3. pre = before**

Base Word   **Definition**

re - __work__ = __rework__ : _to do something over again to make it better_

re - _____ = _____ : _____

un - _____ = _____ : _____

un - _____ = _____ : _____

pre - _____ = _____ : _____

pre - _____ = _____ : _____

Prefixes
#3

> **Main Idea**: A prefix changes the **meaning** of a word.
>
> A prefix is a syllable added to a base word to change its meaning.
>
> Example: "**un**" means not. **un** + happy = not happy

Directions: Add the prefix to the base word. Next, use the prefix to <u>guess the definition</u> of the <u>new word</u>. Use a dictionary to check your answers.

Base Word	New Word	New Definition

1. bi = two

monthly - _____ - _____

_____

annual - _____ - _____

_____

weekly - _____ - _____

2. mis = wrong

understand - _____ - _____

_____

behave - _____ - _____

_____

spell - _____ - _____

3. dis = not

agree - _____ - _____

_____

respect - _____ - _____

_____

obey - _____ - _____

> **Extension:** Select one word from each prefix above. Write each one in a sentence. Underline the prefix.

Prefixes
#4

I. Select a word from the box to complete each sentence.

1. Listen carefully so you don't _____ the assignment.

2. Use a dictionary so you don't _____ the word.

3. The _____ meeting happens in January and July.

4. Students who _____ the rules will have a timeout.

5. On the 1ˢᵗ and 16ᵗʰ he gets his _____ paycheck.

6. If you _____ you might lose a recess.

7. We are still friends even though we _____ constantly.

8. We have PE _____ on Tuesday and Thursday.

9. Don't show _____ to your parents by talking back.

bimonthly
biannual
biweekly
misunderstand
misbehave
misspell
disagree
disrespect
disobey

II. Use a dictionary to look up two (2) words with the prefixes listed below. Write the **base word** on the line. Next, write the **base word** with the prefix together. Finally, write the definition of the word.

Note: When looking up the word, if there is no **base** word, it is not a prefix.

1. bi – to   **2. mis = wrong**   **3. dis = not**

Base Word   **Definition**

bi - _____ = _____ : _____

bi - _____ = _____ : _____

mis - _____ = _____ : _____

mis - _____ = _____ : _____

dis - _____ = _____ : _____

dis - _____ = _____ : _____

Prefixes
#5

Other "Not" Prefixes
non -   im-   in-

Main Idea: A prefix changes the _____ of a word.

I. Match the prefix from the box to each word below. Use a dictionary for help.

1. _____fat   4. _____balance   7. ____sensitive   10. _____stop

2. _____patient   5. _____fiction   8. ____mobile   11. _____perfect

3. _____secure   6. _____accurate   9. ____profit   12. ____expensive

II. Select a word from above to complete each sentence.

1. Because the toys were _____, we all bought one.

2. This is a true story so it is _____.

3. We took a _____ flight from Los Angeles to New York.

4. Calling someone names is very _____.

5. Mom had a _____ muffin because she's on a diet.

6. Bob broke his leg and was _____ for two weeks.

7. We can all go to the show because it is very _____.

8. Because we were so _____ we opened our presents last night.

9. You were _____ when you said two plus two is five.

10. We are all _____ and make mistakes all of the time.

Suffixes
#1

A **suffix** is a syllable added to the end of a word to <u>change its part of speech.</u>

Main Idea: A suffix changes the **part of speech** of a word.

Examples:

sing = verb   sing<u>er</u> = noun   /   beauty = noun   beauti<u>ful</u> = adjective

---

Common Suffixes

1. -ful means "full of" (adjective)   Example: color<u>ful</u> = full of color

2. -ous means "full of" (adjective)   Example: fam<u>ous</u> = full of fame

3. -y means "full of" (adjective)   Example: mess<u>y</u> = full of mess

4. -ible means "capable of" (adjective)   Example: respons<u>ible</u> = capable of
                                                    responding

5. -tion means "the act of" (Noun)   Example: elec<u>tion</u> = the act of electing

6. -ive means "acting in a certain way"   Example: act<u>ive</u> = acting with action
   (adjective)

7. -est means "greatest at" (adjective)   Example: great<u>est</u> = greatest at being
                                                    great.

I. Select a suffix from the box that will change the part of speech of each word below. <u>Bonus:</u> Can you name the part of speech of both the first words and the new words?

New Word	New Word
1. deep - __**deepest**__	9. add - _____
2. faith - _____	10. flex - _____
3. dirt - _____	11. impress - _____
4. nerve- _____	12. wonder - _____
5. sense- _____	13. taste - _____
6. migrate - _____	14. direct - _____
7. destruct - _____	15. big - _____
8. strong - _____	16. stick - _____

Suffixes
#2

Main Idea: A suffix changes the _____ ___ _____ of a word.

-ful	-able	-ous	-y	-ible	-tion	-ive	-est

I. Add the suffixes from the box to the words in parentheses to complete the following sentences:

1. After dinner, the table was _____.   (mess)

2. The _____ students were bothering the teacher.   (talk)

3. We all thought that the movie was very _____.   (enjoy)

4. She was a little _____ about singing on stage. (nerve)

5. My straight A's proves I'm the _____ in the class.   (smart)

6. The trash can was very _____.   (dirt)

7. Be careful because there may be a _____ snake around. (poison)

8. The flood caused the _____ of the city.   (destruct)

9. The waiter was very _____ not to spill the soup.   (care)

10. A _____ person would do all of his/her homework.   (response)

11. There was an _____ for class president.   (elect)

12. Because the back seat was _____, we could all fit in.   (space)

13. Susan is the _____ runner on the team.   (fast)

14. This cup is too _____ to use.   (dirt)

15. Amy did a _____ job on her test.   (miracle)

Extension: Select any five (5) words from the box above. Write them in sentences. Underline the suffix in each sentence.

Suffixes
#3

Main Idea: A suffix changes the _____ ____ _____ of a word.

Common Suffixes

1. -ful means "full of"   5. -tion means "the act of"

2. -ous means "full of"   6. -ive means "acting in a certain way"

3. -y means "full of"   7. -est means "greatest at"

4. -ible means "capable of"

I. The underlined word in the sentences below can be changed using suffixes.
   If you change the word using the suffix, then you need to change the sentence.

   Directions: Rewrite each sentence below using the new word. There is
   more than one way to write each sentence.

   1. The stars in the sky were full of <u>wonder</u>.   (-ful)

      _____**The stars in the sky were wonderful.**_____

   2. We were full of <u>nerves</u> because of the big test.   (-ous)

      _____

   3. My shoes were full of <u>dirt</u>. (-y)

      _____

   4. Heather can <u>create</u> many good pictures.   (-ive)

      _____

   5. That soldier was the greatest at being <u>brave</u>.   (-est)

      _____

   6. Andy has good <u>sense</u>. (-ible)

      _____

   7. The birds will <u>migrate</u> this winter.   (-tion)

      _____

   8. The actor is full of <u>fame</u>.   (-ous)

      _____

Suffixes
#4

Common "People" Suffixes

These suffixes all mean "a person that does something".

-er   **-ar**   **-ist**   **-or**

singer – one who sings   liar – one who lies   typist – one who types

supervisor – one who supervises

I. Change the words below into people by adding **-er -ar -ist -or** . Write the new word. Use a dictionary to check your answers.

1. drive - _____

7. help - _____

2. act - _____

8. instruct - _____

3. beg - _____

9. write - _____

4. cycle - _____

10. garden - _____

5. collect - _____

11. art - _____

6. geology - _____

12. aviation - _____

II. Write five sentences using the person and the action they do. See the sample below:

Example: The driver will drive to the park.

1. _____

2. _____

3. _____

4. _____

5. _____

Suffixes
#5

I. Change the words below into people by adding **-er -ar -ist -or**. Write the new word. Use a dictionary to check your answers.

1. dance - _____

2. biology - _____

3. sail - _____

4. lie - _____

5. farm - _____

6. auth__ - _____

7. dream - _____

8. science - _____

9. play - _____

10. piano - _____

11. supervise - _____

12. guitar - _____

13. dance - _____

14. column - _____

15. select - _____

16. doct___ - _____

II. Use the words on this page to write five sentences about a person and the action they do. See the sample below:

Example: The <u>driver</u> will <u>drive</u> to the park.

1. _____

2. _____

3. _____

4. _____

5. _____

Chapter 9
Review

I. Prefixes

A prefix changes the _____ of a word.

bi-	mis-	dis-	non-	im-	in-	re-	un-	pre-

Directions: Use a prefix from the box above to rewrite the underlined word.

_____ 1. To <u>paint</u> again

_____ 2. Not <u>fair</u>

_____ 3. School before <u>school</u>

_____ 4. Two times a <u>month</u>

_____ 5. To <u>behave</u> badly

_____ 6. To not <u>obey</u>

_____ 7. No <u>fat</u>

_____ 8. Not <u>perfect</u>

_____ 9. Not <u>expensive</u>

_____ 10. Not <u>happy</u>

II. Suffixes

A suffix changes the _____ ____ _____ of a word.

-ful	-able	-ous	-y	-er (person)	-tion	-ive	-est

Directions: Select a suffix from the box that will change the meaning of each
word below. There may be more than one answer.

New Word

1. break - _____

2. create - _____

3. dirt - _____

4. wonder - _____

5. fame- _____

New Word

6. drive - _____

7. deep - _____

8. predict - _____

9. joy - _____

10. stop - _____

Made in the USA
Las Vegas, NV
21 July 2023

75052788R00105